Helen Bullard

The American Doll Artist

Volume II

"Wee" Paulson's "Convention Lady, 1974" illustrates that high moment of doll collecting when the triumphant conventioneer unpacks her recent acquisitions and places them on her display shelves. All the dolls shown are Paulson caricatures of real NIADA artist creations.

The American Doll Artist

Volume II

Helen Bullard

Publishing Athena Company
North Kansas City

First Printing June, 1975

Editorial Consultant Johana Gast Anderton
Photo Reproduction and Typography Complete Composition Service

Standard Book Number 0-89161-006-5

Library of Congress Catalog Card No. 65-22379
Printed in the United States of America

Athena Publishing Company
2016 Clay, North Kansas City, Mo. 64116

to

my Crazy Indian

Preface

THE thirty monographs in this book are based on original research; I went directly to each artist for information about his or her life and work. While it may sound simple, in practice it has taken much mailing back and forth before the story could be told. The life stories differ one from another even more than do the people figures created by these my several colleagues.

As colleagues we are surprisingly congenial and mutually helpful. Each of us works more or less alone and many of us met our first doll artist when we were elected to NIADA, the National Institute of American Doll Artists. Being able to talk shop with a colleague is perhaps the most precious return we receive from our membership in the Institute. The organization came about quite naturally. I had been writing monographs since 1958 on the work of recognized, nationally known artists who were making dolls. At the United Federation of Doll Clubs convention in Buffalo in August of 1962 five of these artists were present with their dolls. We wanted to show them and needed an exhibition room so I went to the hotel manager and arranged to rent a parlor for two hours on Sunday morning. Hazel Snider, a friend and fan of the artists, shared the quick preparations and the eleven dollar rental fee with me. We alerted the artists and at 10:15 a.m. they arrived with arms full of dolls and were directed to the tables we had arranged for their use. But there also arrived seven or eight other dollmakers, mostly unknown to us, who had assumed that they were also invited. With minutes left until opening it was impossible to explain to so many that this was a private showing, so I waved them to tables and window sills in the back corners of the sunny room and we went on to have a wildly successful show.

In order to control future exhibitions it became apparent that we must be properly organized. In a letter to eleven artists I proposed that we organize as a group to hold exhibitions and to meet and undertake such actions as we deemed useful for the group. All but one artist replied enthusiastically. Avis Lee declined; her interest in wood sculpture had replaced her work in dolls. By January, 1963, plans had been made for an organization meeting at my home in Ozone. The best time seemed to be in May following the UFDC Regional Meeting at Watts Bar Resort where Magge Head, Gertrude Florian, Fawn Zeller, and I were to give the program.

On May 12th, sitting on the stone dock at the edge of my pond, we formed the National Institute of American Doll Artists. Our first annual meeting and exhibition was set for August in Los Angeles at the UFDC Convention. The exhibition included the work of the six artists present at the convention, as well as dolls from many absentee members, and was a major event.

The NIADA charter members are Halle Blakeley, Muriel Bruyere, Helen Bullard, Dewees Cochran, Gertrude Florian, Magge Head, Dorothy Heizer, Lewis Sorensen, Martha Thompson, Ellery Thorpe, and Fawn Zeller. All of these artists are represented by monographs in *The American Doll Artist* (1965, Charles T. Branford Company, Boston). So also are Gwen Flather, Grace Lathrop, Gladys MacDowell, and Tamara Steinheil. Other artists, later to become NIADA members, were also included: Betty Curtis, Christine Gorman, Ada Odenrider, and Lita Wilson. Still other artists treated in the earlier book are now deceased or never became NIADA members. The monographs in this present volume are of artists elected after publication of the first volume and not included in it.

Six of our members have died in this interval: Martha Thompson, 1964; Muriel Bruyere, 1969; Grace Lathrop, 1970; Dorothy Heizer, 1973; Gertrude Florian, 1973; and Christine Gorman, 1974. Margaret Hoag, member-elect, died in a plane crash en route to the 1973 Louisville convention at which she was to be initiated into NIADA.

From Seattle, Washington, to Inverness, Florida, from San Diego to Maine and Montreal, we are a close-knit, far-flung group of solitary individualists (except for four couples), professional free-lances, who spend much more than we should with the telephone company because some of our fellow artists are an integral part of our lives.

Our four presidents (Wee Paulson, Astry Campbell, Dewees Cochran, and I) have somehow kept our dedicated individualists working together. In 1974, we accomplished incorporation as a non-profit organization and began working with groups of foreign doll artists who wished to become our associates. The re-organization as NIADA, Incorporated includes a new Associate category for non-American artists. They share all artist privileges except the right to vote.

I am indebted to Astry Campbell for the excellent diagrams of Fern Deutsch's directions for making her special bodies. Our NIADA President, Wee Paulson, has given her complete cooperation as have all our members whose monographs appear herein. Patrons have furnished photographs and data as well as special services. Bernard Kaufmann, always a pillar of strength for NIADA, and Evelyn Perrone have also given special help.

To all of them I tender my sincere thanks.

HELEN BULLARD

Ozone, Tennessee
June 22, 1974

Contents

The American Doll Artist

Volume II

CHAPTER 1

The Artist's Doll

ONLY during the past thirty years have original dolls created by artists begun to appear in sufficient numbers to have an impact. It is easy to understand how the appearance of these dolls coincided with the surge of interest in doll collecting. In the past the artist's doll has usually been made for museums and collectors rather than for children's play. The increased number of serious doll collectors offers a potential market to artists who wish to create original handmade dolls.

The leading early contributors to this movement, Dorothy Heizer with cloth-sculptured figures and Dewees Cochran with latex composition American children, sold their work through New York shops or to well-to-do clients whose personal tastes they served, either in subjects expressing their interests or as portrait dolls of their children. Heizer dolls tended to be gathered into private collections while Cochran dolls were usually acquired singly by individuals in New York and the Northeast.

Later, artists who were also doll collectors entered the field. Also a few dealers, such as Kimport of Independence, Missouri, and Elsie Clark Krug of Baltimore, Maryland, began to deal in handmade artist's dolls. The few hardy souls trying to make all or part of their living in this field were frustrated by a price structure reflecting the attitude of a public that believed the dolls were pin-money piece work turned out by little old women in their spare time. Almost wholly ignored was the artistic value of these dolls. The early dolls of Gertrude Florian dramatically illustrate this casual treatment, for her dolls now bring ten to twenty times what she received for them.

It was not until 1963 when the National Institute of American Doll Artists (NIADA) was organized that the artist's doll began to gain recognition as a work of art and an incomparable interpretation of American culture.

For more than ten years NIADA has held the position that the people figures created by its artists are more than banal consumer products; more, too, than pretty poppets or handicraft items. Since its inception, the Institute has worked to establish the artist's doll as a piece of fine art. The idea of the doll as fine art still has to be defended against skepticism and occasional ridicule, but a growing number of serious collectors, as well as reputable museums that will display them, indicate that NIADA is beginning to make its point.

To complicate the matter, the accepted meaning of the word "doll" connotes a little girl's disposable toy. The finest of these, if they survive long enough to acquire the eclat of the antique, may be collected and valued as historical and sentimental items rather than as aesthetic works. Most of the antique dolls were mass produced and lack the qualities conveyed by the term "artist's doll," that is, a unique work of art created by a trained artist. NIADA would like to discontinue use of the word "doll" and substitute the term "people figure"; however, the preferred designation has not yet been accepted by collectors.

Whether "artist's doll" or "people figure," the definition is clearly stated in the Code of the National Institute of American Doll Artists. To be acceptable a doll must: first, have an artistic intention, an interpretation of personalization from the artist's viewpoint; second, show a high degree of craftsmanship in the control of materials and techniques; and third, have the ability to convey a message through art media to the beholder.

Candidates for membership must present people figures which meet these and additional standards. Each work must be original in concept, and no part may be imitated or reproduced from a mold made by a person other than the artist. The painting must be done and the costuming designed by the artist.

Two categories of artist's dolls are recognized. "Primary" artist's dolls are unique works of carved wood, sculptured cloth, needle-sculptured cloth and felt, or of modeled wax, papier mache, composition, felt, clay, or porcelain. "Original" artist's dolls are defined as reproductions of a primary modeled figure or head, cast from the artist's own mold for poured wax, porcelain, clay, pressed papier mache, composition, latex or any new material adaptable to casting. Such reproductions, which often differ in detail, stand in relation to primary people figures rather as fine lithographs by a painter compare to his water colors and oils.

There is no doubt that dolls created by NIADA standards are extraordinary, but are they, after all, fine art? Dr. Redding S. Sugg has written in a recent biographical article in *Southern Voices* (May-June, 1975), "Helen Bullard and the People Figures," that my own claim in *The American Doll Artist* amounts to a contradiction of Max von Boehn's statement in *Dolls and Puppets,* which opens with the assertion that the doll "has about as much in common with art as the ape has with *Homo sapiens.*" This was a judgment in evolutionary terms because von Boehn studied the antecedents of modern children's dolls through archeology and history in small idols, votive figures, amulets, tomb figures, and fetishes—people figures, that is, with religious or magical values to adults. The modern toy seemed to him a case of arrested development, even of degeneracy as an art object, at best of inconsequential frivolity. Plastic modeling, the beginning of which might conceivably be represented in early people figures, developed into art in sculpture but not in dolls, according to the German writer. "Art, in rejecting the nonessential and the fortuitous, has striven to present a reflection of the soul; the doll has renounced this psychological motive in order to accentuate and intensify the shallow and the external."

In considering the evolution of dolls I presented the artist's doll as a recent mutation dating from about 1930, a period unknown to von Boehn. And, although I did not use the terminology of German idealism as he did, I defined the artist's doll in terms of artistic motive and technique, "inner meaning," and aesthetic impact on the beholder.

For example, serious artists working with dolls in Japan, where there is a tradition of doll art, do indeed "reject the nonessential and fortuitous." If any one thing precludes a doll from consideration as art it is extreme realism; for example, dolls with human hair that cry, talk, wink, wet their diapers, and sport fussily-detailed costumes. Another dubious type of doll is the "effigy" doll which attempts to represent a historical figure, but fails necessarily as a portrait and comes to little more than a romantic or sentimental suggestion of that character.

In order to produce aesthetic impact, the true people figure must express elements of the artist's own national culture and history. This situation in artist's dolls is analogous to that of American artists who grasped from the pivotal 1913 Armory Show in New York the conviction of their own validity in creating American works. Thus they were freed from their old compulsion to imitate English, Italian, and more particularly, French art.

The trend among NIADA artists toward such subjects as culture heroes, legendary characters, and "archtype" dolls representing occupations and ethnic groups is in this direction. It seems apparent that dolls of such subjects are ideally exhibited arranged in groups to show historical or geographical panoramas. In this vein NIADA now has a proposal for support with the Tennessee Arts Commission and the National Endowment for the Arts for a permanent exhibition, "Forty Years of American Children," to be owned by the Tennessee State Museum as a rental property.

Since 1930 when the people figure, created by an artist and executed with professional craftsmanship, began to appear for sale, a ground wave of excitement has been building. NIADA artists have done much to restore to dolls a value for adults at least comparable to that of early idols and amulets. The American artist's doll has an ongoing potential as a means of interpreting the American experience, but it is only in Japan that recognition has been widely accorded the creative efforts of doll artists. We came upon this information about the status of doll artists in Japan through a calendar issued by the Ministry of Foreign Affairs of Japan. An elaborate production, it was filled with color photographs of Japanese dolls and bore this introduction: "A proof of the living nature of this Japanese art, all the dolls illustrated in calendar are creations of artists living today. A number of these artists have been designated by the Government as 'Living National Treasures' in recognition of their superb skill and their contribution to the cultural heritage of Japan."

In Japan the National Institute of American Doll Artists might be a whole bevy of "Living National Treasures," but in the United States it is not. Instead, it is a group trying to demonstrate that here is the beginning of a marvelous way to tell the American story in people figures with personality and vibrance.

CHAPTER 2

Different Media for Different Ideas

ARTIST'S dolls are made in many media. We are sometimes asked, "Why all these different materials for dolls—ceramic, porcelain, composition, papier mache, wax, felt, cloth, latex, and wood? Should every artist work in one perfect material?"

Of course there is no "perfect material"; but more important, just as in sculpture where wood, stone, clay, bronze, sheet metal, paper, plastics, and various combinations of unusual materials are needed to express the exact idea of the artist, so it is with dolls. A message which is admirably expressed in wood can fall flat in sheet metal; a creative idea in clay can be unsuccessful in paper sculpture.

So it is with people figures. Although some artists work in three or four different media, this is usually true only during an experimental period. Most of us settle with a single material and try to solve the many problems involved in using it creatively.

The artist who loves elegance and perfection of detail will choose porcelain, although Dorothy Heizer, for example, used cloth over a modeled face and a body built up of layers of fabric over a wire armature to achieve incomparable elegance.

Porcelain has usually been the chosen medium for the artist whose dolls are reminiscent of the fine French and German bisques of the nineteenth century. All ceramic and porcelain dolls, however, do not need to imitate the frozen prettiness of the nineteenth century lovelies. Porcelain can have strength and energy, as in

Vanek and de Nunez figures, or a new earthiness as in Roberta Bell's Black Americans.

The porcelain and ceramic clays make very nice jointed bodies or, as is more often the case, forearms and lower legs which are attached to cloth or kid torsos. Considerable detail in molding is possible and the resultant figure is proof against all natural enemies, such as heat, cold, moisture, mice, or insects; breakage is the only hazard. Porcelain dolls may also be washed and cleaned. Molding makes possible almost unlimited replicas, each of which may at the artist's pleasure, be gently modeled to a slightly different appearance before the clay is completely dry. Painting may be varied at will; eyes may be naturally painted or of manufactured glass. Some dolls have molded hair; others have wigs of real or synthetic hair. A detailed outline of one procedure used in making miniature porcelain dolls is given on pages 120 through 122.

Gertrude Florian modified the ceramic material in her effort to achieve a superb lifelike natural look and coloring. Her ceramic composition, a secret formula, was worked out to accomplish this end. The wax which she added to the clay softened the surface of the cast piece to convey Mrs. Florian's particular message.

Fawn Zeller, using porcelain, struck out in still another direction. She models the porcelain clay directly and, so far as we know, is the only artist to do this. In this manner she avoids the shrinkage which takes place between the modeling and the fired cast and is able to include fine detail which is not possible with the molding process. Her finished heads are delicate, detailed, and elegant.

Dewees Cochran wanted to create fine play dolls of a sturdy, unbreakable material. She developed a tough lifelike latex composition which is molded much like porcelain although the finishing is more complex. The latex composition has other pleasing qualities; it is not hard and cold to the touch as the clays are, it takes color well, and it has a strikingly natural effect.

The molding techniques of porcelain, with suitable variations, are used in other media such as wax, composition, plastic wood, and papier mache. Artists choose one or another of these for their special qualities. Composition is tougher, less breakable, and can be more realistic in appearance. Wax, a fascinating, malleable, luminous material, can be modeled as a primary or molded. In expert hands it has a lovely lifelike quality. Papier mache has the same advantages as composition but more delicacy is possible, as is evidenced in Betty Curtis's old people. Her special tissue paper mache reproduces the intricate detail of her old people's faces.

Felt as a material handles well and is available in soft flesh tones. It may be seamed and stuffed or stretched over a mold; both methods make possible interesting effects. Stuffed felt is, of course, limited to individually made, or primary dolls.

Fabric is difficult to handle, although it might appear to be the simplest medium of all. The NIADA artists who work in fabric illustrate the range of this medium. Dorothy Heizer perfected the *structure,* which is so difficult in cloth, to such a degree that no doll in any medium has more *presence.* Gwen Flather and Frances Ravca use fabric to delineate old faces with their "needle-sculptured" technique. Most of Bernard Ravca's dolls also are carried out in this medium.

A whole new spectrum of materials such as paper, fabric stiffened with suitable glues, and even more exotic materials has been employed by Beverly Cerepak to achieve special effects. An exciting new era is beginning in this category.

Perhaps at the other end of the media spectrum from porcelain is hand-carved wood. Here each doll is a primary, laboriously carved from a piece of wood. Fred Thompson carves his figures from a variety of woods, each figure one-of-a-kind. My own all-wood, hand-carved dolls are made of horse chestnut wood. We who work in wood must have this material in order to say what we have to say. With knife and chisel we cut away the unnecessary wood to reveal our idea.

Each to his own. Each medium has special qualities and distinct potentials. In a very real sense the medium is the message.

Regardless of the medium used, artists' people figures require much time and painstaking effort to produce. Still it is not the hours expended but the artistic quality which gives them value, *intrinsic* value—the kind of value which puts paintings and sculpture into high-priced Sotheby Parke Bernet auctions. It may take a few years for NIADA dolls to get to those auctions, for they are still too few in number and too closely held by collectors, but artist's dolls already are far beyond the situation of a few years ago when Gertrude Florian would sell one of her exquisite heads for fifteen dollars. So conditioned was Mrs. Florian to the old pin-money prices that nothing we could say to her convinced her that her work of art was worth "real" money.

In a period of rapid inflation, there is little usefulness in discussing the price of anything, but in general NIADA dolls are now commanding prices which come nearer to being fair to the talented creators. While a few very good smaller people figures may be had for about sixty dollars, the price for many cast dolls hovers between one hundred and three hundred dollars. Primary dolls command the same prices or more, although for one-of-a-kind pieces, with all design time chargeable to one figure, this amount will soon be on the increase.

Recognition comes to NIADA artists in many forms; however, our principal showcase is the NIADA Exhibition at the annual convention of the United Federation of Doll Clubs. At this event an average of twenty-five artists exhibit new or favorite dolls at individual tables in a large reception room. For two or three hours the artists show and discuss their dolls with hundreds of conventioning members of Federation.

The Federation's Competitive Exhibition (where recent insurance coverage was a quarter-million dollars) is closed to NIADA; as professionals, NIADA artists do not compete with amateur doll-makers. While this is NIADA's choice and is correct, it does rob the artists of the opportunity to vie for blue ribbons which are dear to the hearts of the newer artists. Smaller competitions such as yearly regional conventions of the Federation as well as arts and crafts competitions are open to them and are sometimes worthwhile. This sort of recognition, because it is received by all the artists, is not noted in the individual monographs, nor is the large body of feature articles which each artist has to his or her credit.

Nearly every NIADA artist has some of his or her dolls in museum collections and a few have entire museums devoted to their work. Movie shorts in earlier years and more recently television programs for the educational channel have been made of several artists' work and methods.

CHAPTER 3

Herbert Vanek

ONE day not long after he had set up his own sculpture studio, Herbert Vanek was asked to make a pouting head for a doll. He had been doing portrait sculpture for many years, but had always worked in life size or larger. He managed to complete the head, but not, he says, "with the greatest distinction." Then he asked his client what this was all about. He learned for the first time that collecting old dolls was a big thing, and that there were also contemporary artist's dolls which are highly prized by collectors.

The idea of making dolls appealed to him strongly so he checked over his skills; he had an inclination for delicate work and fine detail, possibly inherited from his grandfather who was a fine water-colorist of the old German school of minature landscapes in which each leaf and blade of grass is depicted. He had learned the use of the airbrush as a commercial artist, had done mold making and casting in large size heads, and was in control of the small hand brush, so vital for painting eyes, eyebrows, lips, and other detail. He decided to try his hand at dollmaking, for the more he learned of it the more fascinated he became.

To facilitate the switch from large to small figures, he took a crash course in mold making. He had decided on porcelain for his medium because of its delicacy, rich texture, permanence, and adaptability to a wide variety of treatment from the traditional smooth satin finish to a rugged, almost carved effect seldom used in dolls but there at hand for those who wish it.

Combing the library for books on dolls, he came upon *The American Doll Artist* and learned from it the serious work being done by contemporary artists in dolls. He began to write to some of them and received invaluable advice and encouragement, especially from Astry Campbell and Magge Head. Dewees Cochran, who lives near him, became his friend and added greatly to his understanding of his new work.

He chose for his first subject a sculpture of his son Peter at one and one-half years of age. Peter is depicted sitting with one leg extended, the other doubled back. The modeling came quite easily to Vanek but designing the jointed doll so that the limbs would move naturally and look natural in most positions was another matter. To Vanek, this problem is one of the most interesting aspects of designing dolls. The second doll was also of Peter, ten years older, as a "Little Leaguer." There followed the "Modern Troubador"; a "rock guitar player"; "Charlie Chaplin"; Mae West as "Diamond Lil"; "Tom Sawyer"; and a seated portrait of NIADA charter member, "Dewees Cochran," shown working on one of her "Look-Alike" dolls.

Primarily, Vanek wants his dolls to reflect life. He models all parts of the body to make them lifelike and evocative of movement and action. His figures are shown doing something specific; Dewees Cochran working on a doll, Tom Sawyer fishing, the Little Leaguer swinging a ball bat, and the Troubador playing his guitar. Tom Sawyer may be posed to sit, kneel, stand, walk or run, fish, or even paint a fence and smoke a pipe. Charlie can lift his hat, put his hand in his pocket, and hold his cane in different positions. His face is designed so that he looks sad with his head down and droll with his head up. With a rigid material such as porcelain, realism is gained at the expense of flexibility and flexibility at the expense of realism. Achieving optimum balance between these two opposing qualities is one of the most challenging and intriguing problems in conceiving and designing dolls.

As one would suspect, Vanek's style comes through strongly in his dolls. Strong action and expressions full of vigor and life characterize his people figures.

Herbert Vanek was born in Vienna in 1929. His grandfather painted miniature landscapes, was a sculptor, wood carver, and maker of musical instruments. His father was a musician and also painted. In 1939, Vanek went to England as a refugee, lived in a children's home, went to high school, worked in a commercial art studio, and attended Slade School and the Croydon School of Fine Arts. He went to Friends University at Wichita, Kansas, in 1948 and then to the University of Nebraska where he studied art and literature. He was married in his senior year and has two children, Eva and Peter.

He became interested in portrait sculpture while working in an art studio in St. Louis about 1955 and has since completed many commissions. The family moved to the Bay Area near San Francisco in 1960 where Vanek worked as an artist and editor in industry and opened his own studio in 1970. That same year he took his first dolls to the Los Angeles convention of the UFDC, at which NIADA was also having its annual meeting. He met most of the twenty-five artists present and showed the dolls he had finished just prior to the convention. Those five days, filled with interesting contacts and new experiences, reinforced his intention to make dolls. He was elected to NIADA in 1972.

Herbert Vanek with parts and dolls. Tom Sawyer, front left, and Little Leaguer in artist's hand. L to R on case: Charlie Chaplin, Diamond Lil, Troubador, Baby Peter, Dewees Cochran, and Little Leaguer.

Little Leaguer Parts in the Mold.

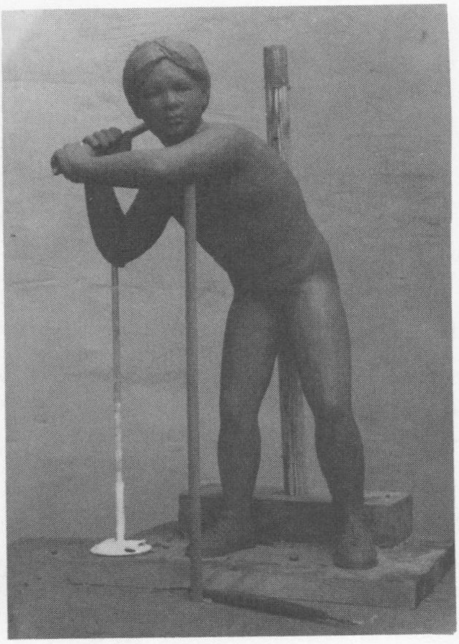

Little Leaguer. Original, modeled in clay, 14 inches.

Little Leaguer. Cast, painted, assembled, ready for dressing. All-porcelain, ball-jointed.

Finished Little Leaguer.

Charlie Chaplin.

Charlie Chaplin Demonstrates his "Universal" Joints.

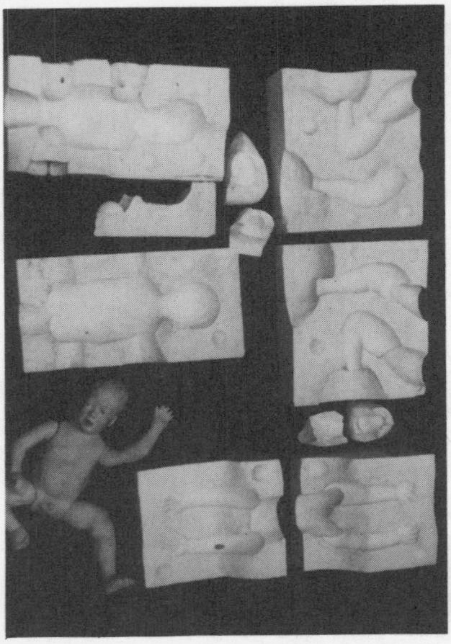

Baby Peter and Molds for Parts.

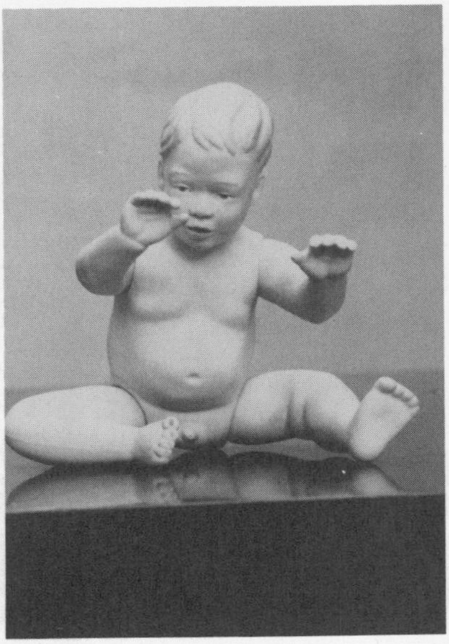

Baby Peter. 7 inches seated.

Modern Troubador. Ready for dressing.

Modern Troubador. Costumed.

CHAPTER 4

Beverly Cerepak

A PERSON'S future is often determined by destiny rather than design and so it was for Beverly Cerepak whose dollmaking began as the result of a school project brought home by her daughter. Her storybook dolls of stuffed fabric, wired with pipe cleaners, had painted or felt eyes and hair of rug yarn wrapped on pencils and set with white glue. A second set used fairy tale characters such as "Snow White," "Little Red Riding Hood," the "Three Bears," and "Cinderella," all of much the same construction but with stronger wires and oil painted faces.

Spurred on by teachers, Cerepak designed about sixty-six dolls, thirty-nine of which were dolls of many nations, all carefully researched. They were of felt, stuffed with cotton and rice (to facilitate posing), and each had a luxurious yarn wig. She experimented with papier mache and liquid rubber but chose instead to make body frames of wire covered with paper and taped in place, mummy-style, for a group of characters which included "Robin Hood," "Peter Pan," "Captain Hook," and "Peter Cottontail."

Later on, to interest her children in United States History, she made thirty-five presidents (adding Nixon later). These were fourteen inches to twenty inches in height and each was appropriately costumed. Materials ranged from papier mache covered with liquid rubber to self-drying clays and balsa wood carvings. Many had taped wire bodies, were painted with enamels, and had Dynel wigs. Each bears an identifying card giving the President's party affiliation, the highlights of his administration, and the names of programs associated with him, such as the New Deal, the New Frontier, and the Great Society.

In 1967 Cerepak went back to nursery rhyme characters and, working with her father-in-law, made scenes such as the *Old Woman in the Shoe,* the *Crooked Man and his Crooked House,* and *Mary and her Lamb.* Cotton, layered with glues and painted with enamels, was used with wired felt bodies. Many had fur eyelashes and beautifully styled hairdos of Dynel. Election year inspired portraits of candidates, including Humphrey, Rockefeller, and Romney, which were made of balsa and pear woods. Mark Twain, Ben Franklin, and Jacqueline Kennedy were also made during this period.

There followed about sixty-six dolls and additional nursery rhyme scenes using glued cottons, papier mache, wood putty, felt, and plastic woods. A new set of United States Presidents (30"-36") was carved of various woods and wood putty with bodies jointed at elbows, knees, and wrists, with movable heads; or bodies of stuffed felt over wire armatures. Legs of redwood and hands of cast plaster completed the figures. Wigs were layered in grooves on the heads.

A complete switch from wood came in the next group of dolls which were formed of foam balls covered with water putty. These manikins for window displays featured such characters as pixies, sea divers, Eskimos, and scarecrows. They followed themes in merchandising and were commissioned by New York merchants who used them as decorative pieces and window displays. In 1971 she began to make ceramic dolls and in 1974 explored the possibility of using porcelain as her principal material.

A normal day for Beverly Cerepak, may very well consist of eighteen or more waking hours. She packs each day with the usual excitement that can be expected from her three children, Mark, Brad, and Kim; develops ideas and coordinates production activity as the toy and novelty designer for Russ Berrie and Company in New York; and approaches her dollmaking with the dedication of an athlete. She looks like a coed and, in fact, she studies biology at Fairleigh Dickinson University, where her husband, John, is Department Chairman and Professor of Business Administration. He is also a well-known author of business publications.

Beverly Cerepak began her basic art training at the School of Industrial Design in Trenton and majored in creative arts at Fairleigh Dickinson. She has also attended many private art courses and seminars. "It seems my family has always been interested in art. Since childhood I can remember art projects in various stages of completion occupying some rather important areas of our home," she writes. "Things haven't changed much; it seems I am constantly experimenting with media and techniques."

Beverly is NIADA's first free-wheeling experimenter in modern materials such as plastics, silicone rubber, plush fabrics, and so on. Her work as a toy and novelty designer keeps her *au courant* of new developments in the commercial field, which she naturally carries over into dollmaking.

Her first show, held at the Paterson Museum in New Jersey, led to others in various libraries, schools, banks, and shopping plazas. She has given lectures and seminars in dollmaking for several large organizations and in 1966 did a full hour program on dolls for educational television. She is a member of the New Jersey Designer Craftsman Guild, the Hobbies Industrial Arts Association of Fairleigh Dickinson, and the Saddle Brook Art Association. She was elected to NIADA in 1970.

Recently she has added a new dimension to her work by developing characters from the "World of Disney" for Kohner's Toy Company and by creating mobile animal figures seen commercially on national television.

Beverly Cerepak

Kim. All-bisque, fully jointed, 14 inches, with four carved teeth.

Nancy. A portrait in jointed bisque made for Kohner's Toys.

Puddin' and Patches. All bisque, jointed, with carved "teeth"; bunnies are "Poms".

Peaches and Patty Cake. All-ceramic baby dolls with molded hair and painted eyes; their little friend is a novelty "Pom Pom" bird.

Sugar-Sugar and Honey-Honey. Heads are styrofoam balls covered with water putty; plastic wood hands and feet; acrylic plush hair; glass eyes on Honey-Honey.

Jack Spratt and His Wife. Who would guess the faces are formed of cotton, then covered with glue?

Lynn. Jointed bisque with her own wooly lamb.

John. Little goose boy is jointed bisque.

Pixie. Jointed bisque with painted bisque wings and carved teeth.

President Washington. 31 inches, jointed body, redwood legs, balsa wood head covered with water putty; plaster hands.

CHAPTER 5

Frances Bringloe

WE first saw Frances Bringloe dolls in the Detroit Children's Museum. Here, we said with excitement, is an artist who is carrying out NIADA's objectives on her own: the expression of American culture through dolls. At Los Angeles the following August we elected her to membership in NIADA.

Her lifelike historical figures are dolls with a purpose. They are used as teaching aids, bringing the flavor and impact of original source material to children in a form easily understood and remembered. Seeing historical groups such as the Lewis and Clark Expedition and typical family groups of important historical periods, children begin to realize that history is made by all people, not just by those who become famous, and that their own time and place are also a part of the story.

For school and library use the various groups are mounted in clear plastic cases and circulated throughout the system. Many Bringloe figures are in museum dioramas which illustrate historical events or daily living. Details of costumes are historically correct since their creator spends much time in researching her subjects.

To achieve lifelike posture and freedom of movement, Frances Bringloe designed wooden bodies in careful scale which she turned on a lathe. By 1966 the work had become so heavy she had to turn some of the processing over to a shop equipped with an automatic lathe. With her carefully worked-out patterns the shop was able to produce her dolls more quickly while retaining the original appearance and quality. She had planned on eventual automatic production and the design of her dolls had been worked out with this in mind. All of the assembly is done in her workshop and is accomplished with tiny steel springs, fishing-tackle swivels, and brass plates. Index carving and similar processes are used for duplication.

Faces and hands are carved from the same Alaskan cedar used for the body parts. The wood is protected with a natural finish, and light touches of color are used in the features and to tint the skin when necessary.

The silhouette of the costume is controlled by choosing fabrics which have *in miniature,* the texture and draping qualities of the original material. Authentic and typical colors are determined by research and achieved by dyeing, scrubbing, or soiling, if required. Decoration is restrained because a small figure can have only essential trimming and each detail is weighed against the final effect. Accessories add interest and enrich the presentation.

When the figures are completed they are mounted on a wooden or plastic base by means of metal inserts in the feet which take screws. Some dolls are displayed in specially designed plastic cases.

Bringloe groups are in the American Museum of Natural History in New York, the Detroit and Indianapolis Children's Museums, Los Angeles Museum of Natural History, Burke Memorial Museum of the University of Washington, Bertha Ball Art Center, Milwaukee Public Museum, Eastern Washington State Historical Society Museum, Kenosha (Wis.) Public Museum, and the public school systems of more than thirty-four states, cities, and counties.

Frances Bringloe, who now lives in Seattle, attended the University of Michigan College of Architecture and Design where she majored in costume and sculpture. She graduated from the University of Washington School of Art in Costume Design. After many years in custom clothes, dress designing and fitting, and teaching design, she began experimenting with dollmaking. Not surprisingly, this interest came to the fore when her two sons were small and she wanted an activity which could be carried on at home. She describes her early doll work best herself:

> During the depression my husband and I spent our summers working in a children's summer camp. As a part of this project the director took groups of older girls to Europe in the winter and also imported wood

carvings from different countries. These carvings were for sale in the camp shop and the children loved them. Many of them depicted various nationalities in typical dress.

An idea began to come to the top of my mind; our own history was certainly as colorful and as fascinating as any, but it had never been presented in a way to appeal to children in their formative years. At this time I was still thinking in terms of stimulating toys. While my boys were babies I played with the idea a little and made some dolls for gifts. These first dolls were cloth with a wire armature and molded plaster face covered with cloth.

My next move was to design a doll typical of the Indians of the Puget Sound area to be sold in toy or gift shops. I did some reading on the people and made a doll which I thought was a "Puget Sound Indian." I was advised to consult an authority, Dr. Erna Gunther, Director of the State Museum and Professor of Anthropology. I sought her out for advice and criticism of my doll. She proved a charming person and a real artist and when she examined my "Puget Sound Indian" she chuckled. "She is a beautiful Samoan but I would like some Puget Sound Indians!"

This experience made me realize that I could not understand a culture after only a few weeks of study. Whenever possible I consult a specialist, either in person or by letter. A person who has absorbed the feel of a culture for a period of years is able to bring much more credibility to a characterization. Such people are always so willing to help that it is a joy to work with them. They are eager to see a serious effort made to portray their special field of interest.

At that time the museum was circulating collections of artifacts to the schools all over the State of Washington to be used in Washington history and social studies classes. The director wanted dolls to show the children the people as well as the artifacts. Here was a whole field of endeavor of which I was totally unaware. It seemed the perfect direction for me. It would involve research, sculpture, sewing, designing, and thinking of children and what makes them tick. In addition, I had already decided that I would probably always be making something with my hands and I was determined to make something useful, not just more figurines, more pots, or more dress designs which try to keep one jump ahead of the trend.

The next objective was to find a suitable material and practical methods of working with it. My husband had a few power tools and I still had those European carvings in my mind. We began to work out figures based on simple turnings, applying the old design principles of making the best use of tools and of your own time and culture. My husband taught me to use the tools myself, insisting that if I were going to design in wood I must work in wood to understand the potentialities of the medium. He was busy with his own affairs (he was an architect), but always gave me help and criticism. Wood was a good choice of material, typical of Puget Sound Indian culture, light in weight (to ease the postage problems of traveling exhibitions), and very durable.

The size of the figures was determined by the container for the collections. A scale of one and one-half inches to the foot, with a six-foot man measuring nine inches tall, was chosen. In time we elected to do most of the processing ourselves, sending work requiring heavy equipment to larger shops to be produced to specifications. Some of the sewing is done outside by help trained in the shop. All special order work is done in the shop, most of it by me. The turned head with which I started has been replaced by finely detailed carvings. The object of making the figures is to have them so perfect in scale and detail that they are thought of as people of the time they represent.

Improving the processing and developing new patterns and jigs to increase production without changing the character of the figures has gone on constantly, especially during the last several years.

Although they are formally known as "historical figures," Frances Bringloe also calls her creations "dolls with a purpose." This purpose she has stated: "There is no need to embellish our past. It is rich in drama and accomplishment. A presentation of the diverse cultures and races which have become a part of America, the conditions which made people leave their homelands and undertake a dangerous journey into an uncertain future, can give the child perspective. The ingenuity and stamina required to build a great country in so short a time will give him pride in his heritage."

Frances Bringloe has had much publicity for her work and has been included in several exhibitions. Recently the Steeg Film Company of New York City came with a crew and elaborate equipment to do a documentary of the whole operation. The film is part of a news-oriented program of short subjects for the United States Information Service. The title is "Vision USA" and will be shown only overseas, probably for television. To illustrate the possibility of the dolls as visual aids, Steeg filmed a fourth-grade history class at the local school. The director was amazed at the children's complete absorption in the dolls and the related lesson in spite of the fact the room was full of television equipment and personnel. The crew also photographed Mrs. Bringloe and her assistant at the studio working at various machines, and hand-finishing and carving original portraits. The director concluded with an interview with the artist and her assistant discussing theory of design and research.

Frances Bringloe is a member of the Northwest Designer Craftsmen (President, 1962 and 1971-1972) and is active in related organizations. She was elected to NIADA in 1971.

Puget Sound Indians. ca. Precontact.

Pilgrims in Sunday Dress. ca. 1620.

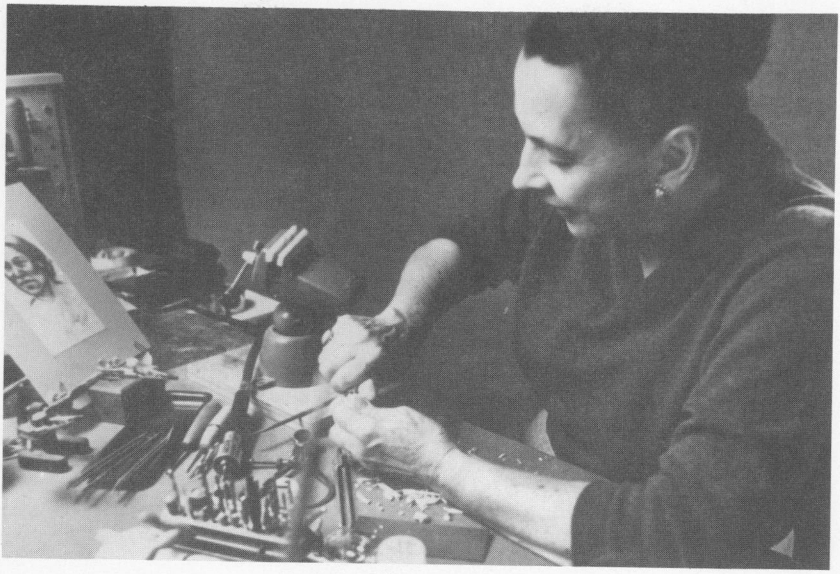

Frances Bringloe at Work.

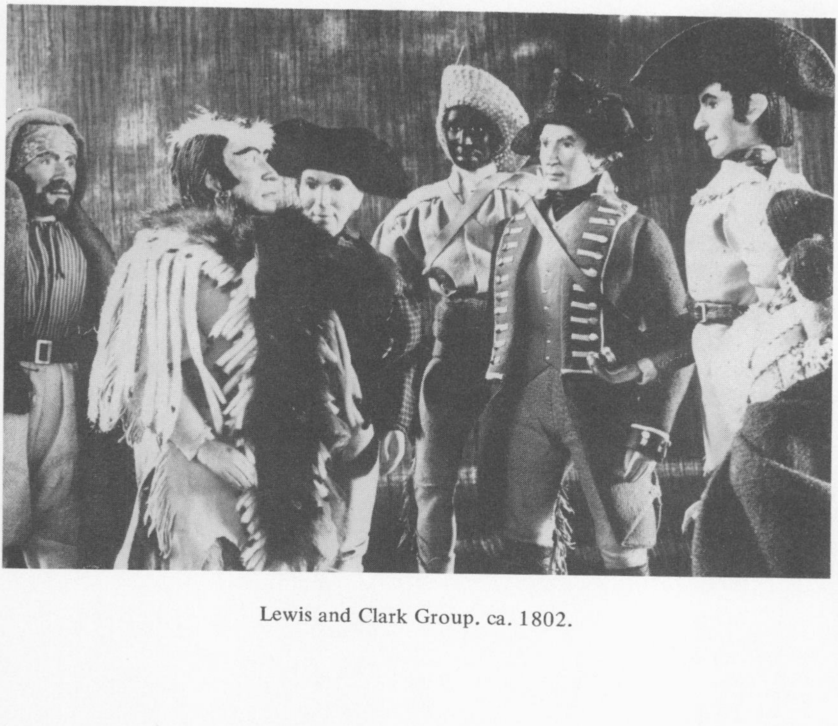

Lewis and Clark Group. ca. 1802.

Klondike Figures. Brainard, Klondike Kate, Soapy Smith. ca. 1900.

CHAPTER 6

Betty "Wee" Paulson

WEE PAULSON lives in an enchanted house. All about her are whimsical figures of elves, children, and angels, vigorously portrayed doing something or other just for fun. The "Five Little Pigs" are going to market, eating roast beef, and saying "Wee, wee, wee," all the way home with such zest that one laughs aloud. On the shelf is a little angel in velvet dress and cloppity sandals announcing Christ's birth to a group of very young shepherds for a truly original nativity scene. Nearby is a blue-jeaned "Tom Sawyer" strolling along with toe bandaged, a slingshot in his pocket and a fish dangling from his fishpole. On a big round table sunbonneted girls, one sitting straight in a ladderback chair in front of a tea table and one swinging from the limb of an apple tree, capture a moment or two of childhood for us.

They are all dolls created by Mrs. Paulson and are known because of her childhood nickname, "Wee," as *Weedidits.* Wee writes:

> I have never done two dolls exactly alike. I love seeing the first one emerge. There is just one rule I use; every doll I create must tell a happy story and bring a smile to children and the young in heart. My work is not limited to storybook dolls, although I love to look up old editions of favorite books and interpret a character down to the most minute detail.
>
> Portrait dolls are another favorite. I call mine *Weesemblances.* I've done most of the neighborhood children, among them "Petey the Cub Scout," "Cindy the rope jumper," and my boy "John" in his cutoff jeans, Snoopy sweatshirt, and sneakers. I also do the neighborhood dogs, including our own Snitzie, the almost-Dachshund.

Her animals are amazing and apparently she stops at nothing; there are dogs, cats, lions, rabbits, deer, and even Babe, the Blue Ox.

Wee Paulson received her art training at Iowa State University where she majored in Applied Arts. Soon after college she married Quentin S. Paulson. They now live in Madison, Wisconsin, with their two daughters and son.

During her art studies Paulson had developed no strong interest in one particular field. After marriage she used her training making curtains and slipcovers, painting portraits of her children, and making dolls, doll clothes, doll houses, and stuffed animals for the children as well as specially designed dresses for her daughters.

About nine years ago she found herself involved in bridge parties and other time-filling activities and decided that this was not what she wanted. In a burst of rebellion she began making elves; some sat on mushrooms or stumps or logs, some pushed wheelbarrows, some carried packages or Christmas trees or toys. These elves were made of felt, partly stitched on the outside with mitten hands and painted faces. "After a few weeks," she says, "I began to separate the fingers, turn the hands, and embroider the faces before painting them. I made sportsman elves for a time, then angels. Storybook characters and portrait dolls of my children and friends followed, but I made no adults or old people until after much experimenting. I discovered that almost any face can be worked out, provided the pattern is cut correctly and the glue and stitches used in the right places." They are all lively characters, meant to evoke smiles of recognition and appreciation.

The sturdy felt bodies of all the dolls are built on wire armatures padded with surgical cotton so that they can be given amusing and natural poses. The nose is a pearl bead, covered with felt, and sewn on the face. Although few of her dolls can be undressed, they will withstand a fall to the floor and may be held, squeezed, and explored by children. Wee makes whatever accessories are needed; she has created chairs, tables, dishes, sporting equipment, baby carriages, rods, reels, and creels, golf clubs, hockey skates, even water and ice. Her children believe that with her sewing machine and trusty jackknife she can make anything and she probably can. One never knows what will happen with tools in the hands of a person with an elfin sense of humor and a lively imagination. Her signature is a small mushroom with *Weedidit* across the top.

When a few years ago she was asked to do a portrait doll of Wisconsin's Governor Warren P. Knowles for his inauguration, she was concerned about giving such a prominent and distinguished person a pearl bead nose without insulting him. But of course he was pleased with his doll.

Because she loves to tackle a new problem, she cuts each doll and animal directly from the material with no pattern at all. She seldom uses a ruler but relies on her own sense of scale.

The serious side of the operation involves hours of research at the library or a special trip to see a particular object, such as a rolltop desk, a World War I hat, a Yorkshire terrier, rare orchids, antique carriages, or a uniform and emblem of a particular airline.

Since being voted into NIADA in 1968, Wee Paulson has given many talks and doll exhibitions in which she has shown not only her own dolls but also many from her growing collection of NIADA artists' dolls. She was East Coast Vice President of NIADA, 1971-73, and President, 1973-75. Her big project has been the incorporation of NIADA and its registration as a non-profit organization.

The Four Seasons–Spring.

The Four Seasons–Autumn.

"Here!"

Happy Hanukkah.

Follow the Star.

Warm Feeling.

Red Loves Hattie.

Wee Paulson with Convention Group, Little Leaguer, and the Uglies.

CHAPTER 7

Herta Forster

HERTA FORSTER was born in Darmstadt, Germany, to a family of official artists. Her grandfather, Professor Wilhelm Horst, a painter, sculptor, and avid art and antiques collector, took care of the paintings belonging to the Hessian grand dukes in their various castles in Germany. He also worked as a restorer for the Hesse Landesmuseum in Darmstadt. Later Herta's father stepped into *his* father's shoes.

After a very sheltered childhood as an only child, she spent her teen years in turmoil of the horrors Hitler had set in motion. She studied to be a kindergarten teacher in order to avoid being drafted into the army. In September, 1944, her parents' house and the neighborhood were bombed by the Allies and everything was lost except the clothes they were wearing.

The period following the war was full of hardship. The destruction of the banks and their records meant that there was no money and there was no work for painters or restorers. Herta made dolls and teddy bears, using rags and old draperies given her by lucky friends who had not been bombed out. In this way she contributed to the family income. The small village where her family found temporary shelter was about fifteen miles from Darmstadt. In 1946, when times became somewhat more stable (money in the banks had been devalued to 10%), she went to art school for two years, studying painting, sculpture, anatomy, and other fine arts subjects.

In the village she met Rudolf Forster who emigrated to the States in 1929 and worked for the United States Military Intelligence as an investigator. In 1948, after they were married, he was transferred to California where they have lived since. Her husband became an immigration investigator and after four years of outside work Herta Forster became a homemaker with time to go back to the dolls which were her great interest.

Forster's dolls are mature people, full of humor and satire. They are solid personalities who usually exhibit frailties and foibles. Many things influence her point of view including, of course, her experiences during the war years and the final catastrophe of being bombed out and homeless. Her view of life was conditioned by the time spent with her people under ultimate stress and their reactions to events which destroyed their chosen ways of life.

She was also influenced by the illustrated verse stories of a well-known German humorist and satirist, Wilhelm Busch. As a child she did not entirely understand the allegories involved, but the ink drawings were very clear to her and she spent so much time with the huge books that she knew the words and drawings almost by heart.

Since 1961, when she began devoting most of her time to dolls, she has made ninety-two humorous or satirical dolls and many stuffed animals, puppets, marionettes, and felt child dolls. Her particular love is the satirical figure in period costume, which she researches with great care. All satirical figures are one-of-a-kind pieces.

While her medium is felt (originally inspired by her admiration for the work of Kathe Kruse), the heads of the humorous and satirical figures are modeled individually of wood composition and painted. For hair she uses a variety of materials, such as fake fur, crepe, vicuna wool, synthetics, and human hair. The bodies of felt are constructed over a wire armature, as are the arms and legs. Arms and fingers are hand-stitched. She designs and makes the costumes and accessories, including animals and furniture when needed. Sizes vary from twelve inches to twenty-two inches, fourteen inches being her favorite size. Although she prefers not to work on order, she is open to suggestions in working out new figures.

In 1972 Herta Forster illustrated a children's book, titled *Greg Finds an Egg,* using her own characters, animals, and backgrounds. The book, by Sarah Keyser, was done in color and was published by Platt and Munk. Forster was elected to NIADA in 1970.

Gladys and Tyrone. Scene from TV's "Laugh-In", 1969.

Herta Forster with her Pilgrim Woman and Bawdy 1880 Couple Dancing.

Biedermeier Pair. ca. 1830.

"Goodness, What a Beak!"

Rococo Lady, Feathered Friend, and Lady in Fur Cape.

Children in felt. 13 inches.

Pedlar Woman and Rainy Weather.

CHAPTER 8

Astry Campbell

ONE of the most curious things about artist's dolls is that artists are often unaware of their existence. Astry Campbell's art education and experience were top-drawer, New York style; however, it was only when she was brousing in a Palo Alto doll shop that she discovered dolls existed in the field of art. She bought a doll, a portrait of a young girl, and only years later learned it had been made by Dewees Cochran.

Ideas raced through her head; could *she* make an original doll? Her husband encouraged her; with all that art training, why couldn't she? She was a sculptor, she had worked with clay and ceramics, and had studied mold making under Ettore Salvatore while in college.

She chose to make a contemporary fashion doll for her first figure. Since she had been a Powers model, her concept of a fashion doll was a manikin, elegant and professional. Contemporary in style with basic elements of the human body idealized and simplified, her dolls are conceived as total functioning units with all parts movable. The shoulder head and lower limbs of her early dolls were procelain on a fine kid body and measured twenty-two inches in height. The toy buyer at I. Magnin, to whom she showed her first completed doll, gave her an order and her first dolls were shown by that fashionable shop. Before she could design another doll she moved with her husband and three children back to New Jersey and set up her first studio in their new home. "Becky," a nine-inch toddler, intended for a play doll, had a soft felt body and legs with porcelain head and arms. Her brother, "Ricky," with the same construction, was modeled after Astry's son. She sent photographs of "Becky" to I. Magnin and back came an enthusiastic letter requesting rights to sell "Becky" west of Arizona and would she send them five hundred dolls before Christmas? After she recovered from the shock, she regretfully declined.

Her next design, "Alice in Wonderland," was a fully jointed bisque doll and was copyrighted. Astry, now seriously involved in original dolls, decided to make each design a limited edition so as to free herself for new creations. In 1974 her Alice won the first place award in the sculpture category at the Summit (N.J.) Art Center Exhibition. Her "Baby Lisa," is a fully jointed porcelain doll representing a three-month-old baby. The expression catches that brief moment when the baby may either laugh or cry. The doll was purchased by the Smithsonian Institution for exhibition in its traveling exhibition of American dolls.

As a child in New York City, Astry loved drawing and painting, but was made to study the piano. Her parents and her piano instructor hoped she would qualify for admittance to the High School of Music and Art but Astry had other ideas. She made up an art portfolio, took the two-day examination, and was accepted as an art student at the high school. After graduation she spent two summers working as a draftswoman for an architect. She had wanted to attend Cooper Union or Pratt, but was sent to Barnard College where she managed to enroll in every available studio course and took her B.A. in fine arts. Sculpture was her main interest; she studied with Aronzio Maldarelli whose approach was the simple modern classic one. Later she was a student of Hugo Robus from whom she learned fluid movement in sculptural form and also studied painting with Reginald Marsh. Then her interest in simple primitive form led her to an M.A. degree in the field of Black African sculpture.

A year of teaching, a few years in the "bull pens" of several advertising agencies, and a stint as assistant art editor of the staff of *American Girl* Magazine kept her busy until she married Arthur Campbell who was then a junior in medical school. Travel with their three children included a period in Heidelberg, Germany, where Dr. Campbell was assigned to the hospital at USAREUR Headquarters. Not wishing to do graduate work in art history at the University of Heidelberg because of its heavy emphasis on German art, Astry became a psychology major and after two and a half years of study worked as a clinical psychologist for the United States Army.

The Campbells then settled in New Jersey where Astry discovered a local doll club and became a member. At the UFDC convention in Boston in 1967 she met Dewees Cochran who had created the first original doll she had ever seen. Campbell was elected to NIADA in 1968 and from 1971-73 she served as President. She designed the NIADA logo, or trademark, in 1970 when she redesigned the Institute's brochure, letterhead, certificate, and other papers. During her presidency she submitted the NIADA trademark to the United States Copyright Office and researched the possibilities of incorporating NIADA as a non-profit organization.

Astry Campbell With Dolls.

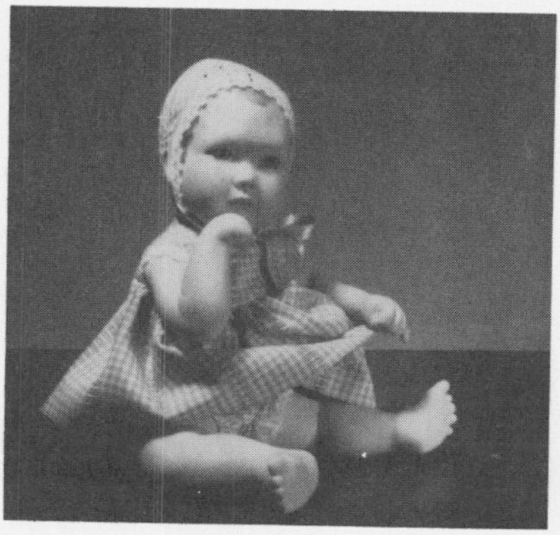

Baby Lisa.

Becky.

Fashion Doll.

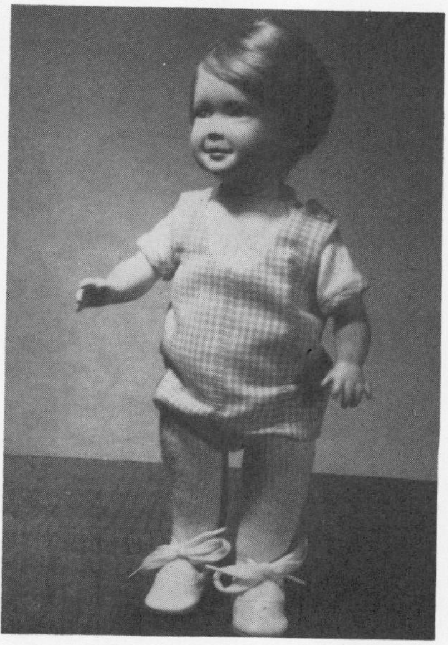

Ricky.

CHAPTER 9

Joyce Stafford

AT the age of eleven Joyce Stafford designed and sewed her first dress from an old sheet. By the time she was sixteen she was making her own clothes and designing some of them. She was still in high school when her first sculpture, a bust of Joan of Arc, won a prize. She went on to Denver University where she majored in art and earned a master's degree in education. While working for her college expenses she picked up skills in ceramics and leather work.

After three years of teaching kindergarten, she married John Stafford and continued to teach while their son was an infant. When he started school she quit teaching and used her extra time in restoring antique dolls which she had begun collecting. Their scarcity and high price, however, caused her to consider making her own. It took her two years to find the best materials and techniques required to duplicate the fine antique process of the dolls she admired and to locate the sources of porcelain, china paint, eyes and lashes, leather, and other needed items.

She named her first porcelain doll "Ada Lou" after her mother and her second, "Little Ruth," won a blue ribbon at the California State Fair. A Jackie Coogan, as "The Kid," followed and is still one of her favorites. She went on to portray William S. Hart, the early movie cowboy, and a variety of other characters.

While she works well with all subjects, Stafford is especially gifted in interpreting children, perhaps because of her ten years as a teacher. She chooses her models from photographs of famous people and from family or friends, and works out her designs with great skill and a stubborn desire for excellence. Her dolls' heads, hands, and sometimes legs and bodies, are of high-fired porcelain. Flesh tones are permanently fired china paint. The wigs are hand-sewn and the eyes are of glass. The clothes and leather shoes are designed and sewn by Mrs. Stafford. The bodies are tightly stuffed with dacron to produce the firm yet soft feel that is unique with her dolls.

Among Joyce Stafford's many interests is the designing and making of silver and turquoise jewelry. She has been a collector of Indian jewelry since 1949 and has taken classes in jewelry making; she started making her own silver and turquoise Indian designs when prices of the authentic pieces began to increase. She also has an extensive collection of movie memorabilia from the early silent film up to the present from which she researches her movie star dolls. Her large collection of children's books furnishes ideas for her child dolls.

Because Joyce Stafford's greatest joy is in creating new dolls she generally restricts production of any doll to ten or fewer so as to allow herself more time for new dolls. She was elected to NIADA in 1969 and is currently West Coast Vice President. She lives in Holliston, California.

Joyce Stafford with portrait doll of Great-Aunt Mary Goodlet.

Buttercup. 13 inches.

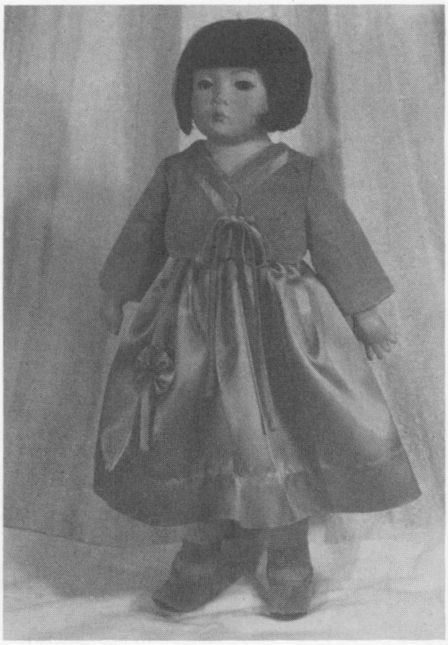

Sue Ling. Korean toddler. 18 inches.

Becky. 13 inches.

Dulcy. 26 inches.

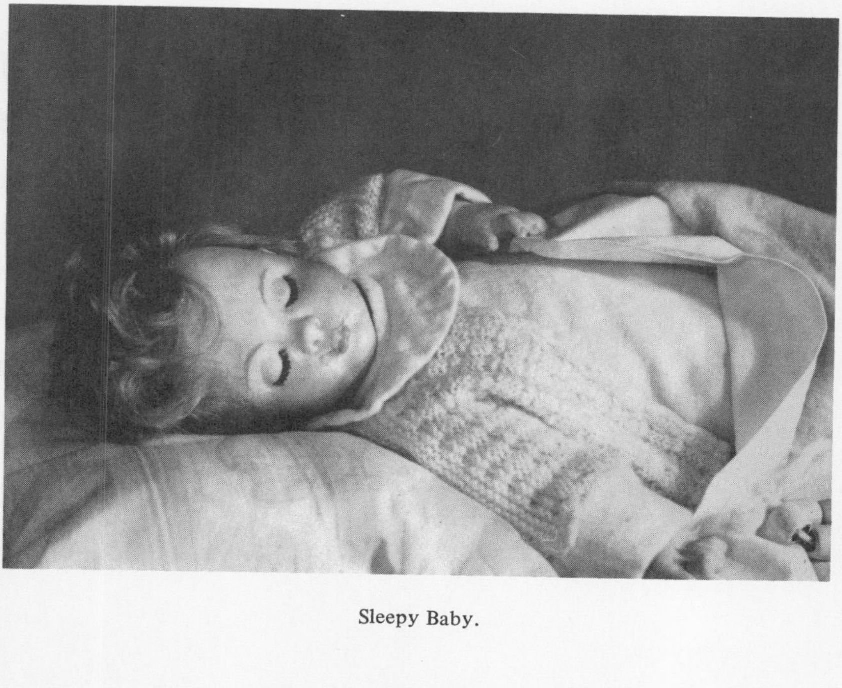

Sleepy Baby.

The Primm Family. Small dollhouse dolls.

Dolls of the Month. L to R: May, April, June, July.

CHAPTER 10

Suzanne Gibson

ONE sunny morning in 1972, Suzanne Gibson woke up with a great new idea. Rushing to her studio, she threw a handful of modeling clay on her modeling stand and in five minutes her fingers had patted and pressed a new and exciting little girl face out of the clay. That elegantly simple face with a truly modern feeling, free of sentimental prettiness yet full of appeal, is a departure from traditional doll faces. The "Kalico Kids," four girls and a boy, have proved a tremendous success. Dressed in nostalgic printed cotton dresses and sprigged aprons or pinafores; the little boy in denim jeans and striped shirt with fishpole and can of worms; they are instantly appealing. They have been advertised in *House Beautiful* and also sell through exclusive showrooms in Los Angeles, San Francisco, Denver, Dallas, and the World Trade Center in Houston. Handsome note cards, color photographs, and large posters featuring the "Kalico Kids" have been made up and sold in all five designs.

Gibson's success came about after years of struggle for she is characteristically overextended. She has always loved dolls and had tried making some of her own, carving the first few out of wooden dowels with a razor blade. When she discovered Xacto carving tools, she carved about a dozen dolls out of soft pine and costumed them elaborately. After a long interval she tried sculptured cloth dolls and then became interested in making dolls with ceramic heads. She took a course in puppet making and then one in ceramic modeling and molding. Later, she switched to porcelain, making a number of little girl dolls after she had completed a successful portrait of her mother as a little girl.

Besides teaching ballet, Suzanne Gibson was also trying to set up her own business of designing and making elegant dresses for little girls. Some years earlier she had designed little girls' party dresses for Marshall Field & Company and Saks Fifth Avenue. She was sure she could find good markets in California and decided she would make dolls to help finance the dress project.

The little girl dolls which she produced in porcelain in 1966 were sold through I. Magnin of San Francisco. For two years this shop had window displays of Gibson dolls; later she began selling directly by mail.

Suzanne Gibson was born in Pocatello, Idaho, and grew up in Minneapolis where her father, as choreographer and ballet master, directed the Twin Cities Opera Company ballet. She spent her childhood watching rehearsals and joined the company at an early age. She and her seven siblings were dance-crazy and four of them, including Suzanne, became professional dancers. Later she and two of her sisters toured the country, performing musical comedy in theatres and at fairs. She wrote, produced, and staged shows in Kansas City, Toronto, Buffalo, and Minneapolis and in 1956 she opened the Ecole de Ballet in San Leandro, California.

She wrote and directed a three-act children's ballet, "Pinocchio," which earned her an official invitation from the Italian State Tourist Office and officials of the city of Pitoia, the home of the original Pinocchio, to perform at one of the annual festivals. In 1966 she closed the school to devote her time to dolls. She taught classes in Dollmaking Design for two seasons at Cabrillo College in Aptos, California. The second class description read: "A previous class was attended by completely inexperienced dollmakers who exhibited finished dolls this spring at Miss Gibson's Capitola shop. Each student began by sculpting her doll's head, arms, and legs in clay. Then came making the molds, designing, sewing and stuffing the bodies, pouring the molds, firing, painting and refiring, setting the eyes, designing the wigs, and finally, styling and making the clothes." At the end of the course Suzanne held open house to show her students' dolls and her own collection to visitors. She was elected to NIADA in 1967.

In 1970 Suzanne married Marcello Storti who had lately come from Italy where he had taught art history. With a master's degree in art from the Royal Academy of Art in Naples (1970), he had planned to teach art in California. Instead, he began working on original dolls of his own. He also shared the responsibility for Suzanne's various endeavors. She was making more and more dolls and had resumed her ballet classes which soon grew into the Santa Cruz Civic Ballet.

Besides the "Kalico Kids," and the little girls, Gibson's dolls include fashion dolls of various periods, including Gibson Girls and Godey Ladies, babies and babies with nannies, some portraits, a "Twiggy," and a striking group of four ballerinas, Pas de Quatre, which are conceded to be among the best ever made.

Little Boy in Sailor Suit.

Sarah Jane.

Gibson Girl.

Gibson Girl with Little Girl.

Little Girl.

Gibson Girl Shoulder Head.

Suzanne Gibson and Ballerinas.

CHAPTER 11

Madeline Saucier

OUR Canadian member's childhood was very different from that of the rest of us. It was highlighted by summers spent in her maternal grandparents' seigneurial manor of thirty-three rooms on the Gaspe Penninsula where her mother and eighteen siblings had grown up. In the attic were trunks of beautiful dresses for Madeline and her cousins to try on during rainy days. Years later she thought ruefully of those dresses when she needed period materials for doll costumes. The great estate, with its extensive timberlands and farms kept by tenant farmers, was supervised by her grandfather who also ran a pulp import business, traveled often to Europe, and served as consul in Quebec for Sweden and Norway. In those days few consuls came from the countries they represented. Many celebrities were entertained at the manor and the talk was often of world affairs.

The nineteen children studied with a governess until they left, one by one, for colleges and convents in eastern Canada. Some became writers and poets, some men of affairs, and several cultivated artistic tastes. They and their descendants made a large connection and Madeline Saucier usually "knows somebody" in all areas of Canadian life.

Madeline Saucier made her first small dolls of wax during a long convalescence before she was eight years old. A collection of small dolls given to her had to have additions and she made them using wired bodies of cloth and making their costumes.

After being tutored at home in Montreal, she entered convent where, on doctor's orders, she spent much of her time on art studies in sculpture, modeling, and painting. She was the youngest student to win the "Ecole des Beaux Arts" Award for a portrait in oils. After convent she attended the Institut Pedagogique in Montreal and later the Art School of the Montreal Museum of Fine Arts for drawing, portrait, and anatomy. Then she studied sculpture and modeling at Sir George Williams University and did further portrait work under Adam Sheriff Scott of the Royal Canadian Academy of Arts.

She opened her own studio, teaching drawing and portrait painting while experimenting with dolls of wood, papier mache, French needle-modeling, wax, composition, cloth, and felt. She designed during this period for Raphael Tuck & Company, New York, and later for the Wilkinson Company, New York, mailing in her designs. In 1938, her bronze bust, "Grape Woman," was exhibited by Marcus and Company, New York. From 1939 to 1946 she headed a Red Cross group and continued to experiment with doll techniques.

In June, 1947, she married Major Andre Morin, a military attache in Paris, and in 1953 a son, Andre, was born. After a lengthy illness, Major Morin died in January, 1961.

In the ensuing period Madeline Saucier did a variety of art work and soon decided to become an artist in dolls; there were none of stature in Canada at that time. She concentrated her studies on relevant subjects, plus a special course in applied arts. In 1963, she was commissioned to make a series of seventeen dolls dressed in national costumes of various countries for a fashion show called "Fashion is International," sponsored by the Fashion Group of America. This series was reproduced for Jordan Marsh of Boston, with other special dolls, in 1966.

In November, 1965, she had her first one-person show in the Fine Arts Center at Stewart Hall, Pointe Claire, on the Island of Montreal, with more than thirty dolls on exhibition. At Expo '67 in Montreal she showed about thirty-five dolls, many of which were portraits of contemporary Canadian children. In November, 1969, she had an exhibition of all her dolls at the Montreal Museum of Fine Arts.

She collaborated with the University of Ottowa Department of Psychology and Education for a monograph on "Doll Art" and with the University of Montreal Department of Anthropology on creating dolls. In 1964, some of her dolls were donated by the Montreal Historical Society for permanent display at the New York Military Museum; the same year Walt Disney commissioned some of her Canadian dolls for Disneyland at Anaheim. Her work is also in doll collections at McGill University in Montreal and in private collections in Europe and America.

She has made numerous major television appearances in Canada, three of which were coast-to-coast, and one in Burlington, Vermont (1964). In 1971 she made a half-hour educational television program for use in Canada and the northern United States. Many newspaper and magazine articles have covered her work and the various exhibitions. A radio interview by a Belgian radio reporter was taped in French for distribution to Belgian radio stations.

The faces of Saucier dolls made since 1963 are of a special formula of hardened felt with hand-painted features and inserted eyelashes. The bodies are fully wired and are covered with cloth or felt. Since 1966 all her dolls are commissioned portraits, many represent living children. Most of Madeline Saucier's dolls are limited editions which are copyrighted and registered as works of art. The subjects are so often Canadian that she is generally considered to be the official Canadian doll artist.

Saucier is an artist member of the Montreal Museum of Fine Arts. She was elected to NIADA in 1968 and is now an Associate Member.

Madeline Saucier with "Woman of Quebec," from the Grevedon lithograph on wall.

Farm Boy.

L. to R. Cantiniere, Canadian Beaver, Little Girl in Sunday Best, Drummer. Seated: Suzanne.

L. to R. Madeleine de Vercheres, Red River Girl, Habitant Woman.

L to R: Standing, Suzanne, Mountie, Lili, Pierette; seated, Canadian Snow Baby and Fanchon.

CHAPTER 12

Roberta Bell

WHEN Roberta Bell made Black American dolls to use in teaching history to her fourth grade class, she did not know that she was beginning a whole new career. She knew she could dramatise black history for her students with dolls, but was surprised when adults showed an interest in her "Famous Black Americans" and wanted to hear their stories. Since her retirement a few years ago, she has created a unique group of dolls which she exhibits all over the country. *Ebony* magazine carried a feature article on her dolls in May, 1972, which resulted in numerous invitations to exhibit and speak.

She was born in Nashville, Tennessee. Her father was a portrait artist and sculptor from whom she learned in daily contact. She chose, however, to study in the fields of education and social work, taking her A.B. at the University of Kansas and her M.A. at Northwestern University in counseling and guidance. Along the way she continued her interest in art, attending many workshops and seminars in art and ceramics and conducting consistent independent research and experimentation. In addition to teaching elementary school, she worked as Y.W.C.A. administrator and counselor and as a supervising vocational counselor for the Chicago Department of Welfare. Born I. Roberta Bell, her name remained unchanged after her marriage to Solon C. Bell, whose work in organizing the first labor union among dining car employees on the Union Pacific Railroad has been widely recognized.

Her father had deplored the fact when she was a child that she had only white dolls. Once he removed the pink and white bisque head and hands from a fine new doll and modeled black ones to replace them. This doll was much loved but a large special doll kept since childhood formed the nucleus of her now extensive doll collection which includes many black dolls among the usual white ones. Her first effort at making dolls came in the early forties when she used homemade papier mache, oven-hardening clay, and cloth. She made and sold many rag dolls during the war years using McCall patterns. At a ceramic show she bought some doll molds, including some by Magge Head made by Bell Ceramics Company. She took workshops in mold making, feature painting, and the handling of clay and molds. Porcelain became her medium and with an "apartment" kiln she was on her way. She soon began creating her own originals and chose the general subject of "Famous Black Americans" remembering that as an elementary school teacher she had wanted to make history come alive for her fourth-graders.

Dr. George Washington Carver, the great authority on peanuts, their culture and use, was the subject for her first black doll. When she took the doll to school, teachers as well as pupils were enraptured. She had even caught the slump in his shoulder, a familiar sight as he walked on the campus at Tuskegee Institute in Alabama. She didn't know about the slump, but her subconscious must have included it. She had once seen Dr. Carver when she was a teenager and she certainly had a feeling for his personality.

The success of her first doll encouraged her to create dolls representing other Black leaders: Mary McLeod Bethune, Harriet Tubman, Sojourner Truth, Paul Laurence Dunbar, Crispus Attucks, Jean Baptiste Point De Sable, W. C. Handy, Dr. Dan Williams, Frederick Douglass and his wife, Anna Murray Douglass, an Ashanti Queen Mother, and Dr. W.E.B. DuBois as well as many lesser figures in Black history. She is working on an African family which includes grandparents, parents, and a little boy and girl.

Before attempting a new character, Bell does a great deal of research in an effort to understand the character, emotions, beliefs, and philosophy of the subject to the best of her ability. When she feels she is ready she models the heads in plastilene, attempting a reasonable likeness which, in later operations of molding and cleaning, she refines to the exact likeness she desires. The color of the porcelain is amazingly different for each character and all shadings seem to have great validity and naturalness. She handles the porcelain artistically to produce a rough and strong, rather than traditional smooth bisque, effect. The head and hands are molded of the colored porcelain with painted features and the rest of the body parts are cloth, stuffed with sawdust. Wigs take special treatment and Mrs. Bell has worked out her own techniques using "poodle cloth" or mohair, with proper haircuts being given to the men after the wigs are in place. Costuming is carefully designed and made to suit the style and period of the subject. All dolls are copyrighted, with the name incised above the copyright mark.

Roberta Bell is presently working on a commission from the National Association of Fashion and Accessories Designers for a series of fashion models. These dolls will be costumed by the members in fashions dating from 1865 to 1970. The series is planned as a permanent memorial to Mary McLeod Bethune.

Roberta Bell was elected to NIADA in 1970.

Dr. George Washington Carver. The Peanut Wizard.

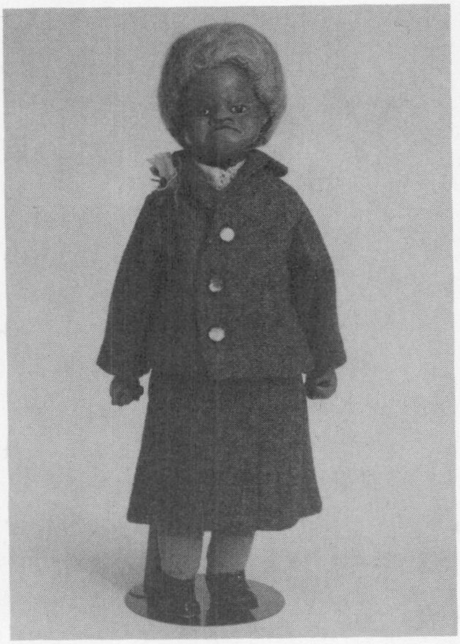

Mary Bethune. Educator, humanitarian, and advisor to President Franklin Roosevelt.

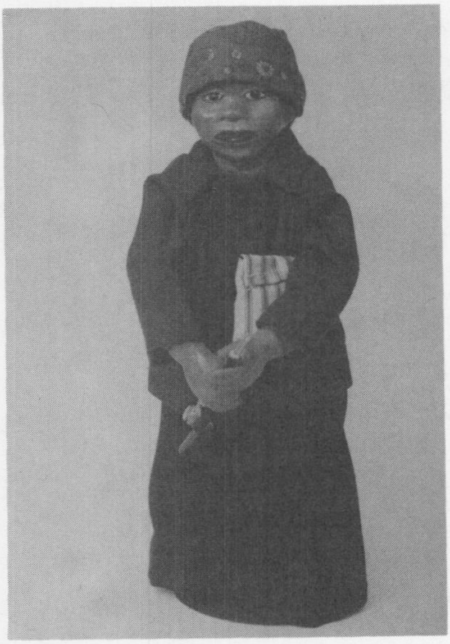

Harriet Tubman. The "Moses of Her People."

W. C. Handy, "Father of the Blues."

Sojourner Truth. Abolitionist, suffragette, born in slavery.

Paul Laurence Dunbar. "Poet of the People."

Jean Baptiste Point de Sable. Trapper and fur trader of Chicago.

Cristus Attucks. Revolutionary Patriot-Martyr.

Roberta Bell stuffs a doll body. Front, L to R: Solon C. Bell, Ashanti Queen Mother, Sojourner Truth, Dr. George Washington Carver, Matthew Henson.

Roberta Bell. Painting features on cast heads.

CHAPTER 13

Rose Sullo

Rose Sullo made her first dolls while a student at Cooper Union in New York. There were a dozen or more, all of them caricatures. Although she had planned to do a whole series of dolls, marriage to Joseph Sullo and the arrival of their three children interrupted for a while. In 1957 her eight-year-old daughter, Susan, was ill and bedridden. Rose had used every idea she could summon to keep the child amused when she remembered the old dolls stored in the basement. By a coincidence she heard of a doll and hobby show soon to be given by a local club. Full of excitement, she enlisted the help of Susan to clean and freshen the dolls so that they could be entered in the show. Susan loved helping with the mending, repairing, and redressing and soon forgot her aches and pains.

All the while Rose Sullo was bursting with new ideas for dolls she could make. She could hardly wait to get a coat hanger and her tools and go to work. First came the organ-grinder and his monkey which she remembered so fondly from childhood. This work grew into a long list of figures, all caricatures, but gentle, loving ones with never a dirty dig or a mean thrust to any of them.

Growing up in Queens in a mixed neighborhood, she learned to love the organ-grinders, the street peddlers, the gardeners of nearby estates, the blacksmith, and the butchers, as well as the people she observed at beer parties, songfests, and clambakes. Now long gone, these people are immortalized in her loving caricatures. Many of the figures have been retained in her private collection which she uses to illustrate her lectures for charitable functions at local clubs. Newspapers, regularly carry reports of these talks and Mrs. Sullo has a fat clipping file.

Rose Sullo models the head, hands, legs, and feet, including shoes, of self-hardening clay directly on a heavy wire armature which is screwed into a wood base providing support for the body. The arms are made on copper wire with fingers of very fine copper wire. Generally she works from photographs, although sometimes she uses herself or anyone available to obtain a desired expression. Portrait dolls are done from photographs only.

The clay takes careful handling as it must dry from the inside out and this can only be done slowly. The work is exposed gradually to the air by using a plastic bag to regulate the amount of exposure. When the doll is thoroughly dry it is painted with oil paints. After the paint is thoroughly dry, the frame is wrapped with strips of cotton until the figure is shaped to suit the character. A cotton knit material goes over the figure as a sort of underwear and it is then ready for costuming. Because the figure is already screwed to the base, only blouses, shirts, and jackets can be made separately and slipped over the doll. If the arms are holding an object, all the garments must be attached piece by piece, a slow and exacting procedure. A doll takes about a month to make because of the drying time of the clay and the oil paint. Early works had modeled eyes while the later ones have inset glass eyes. Sullo's dolls are usually about twelve inches tall and are one-of-a-kind, except as noted in the catalog.

Rose Sullo's greatest moment came in 1972 when President Nixon agreed to accept her figures representing President Nixon and Chairman Mao of China shaking hands. She has a gracious thank you letter from the President acknowledging her gift. A photograph of the pair appeared on the February, 1973, cover of *Doll News,* the quarterly of the United Federation of Doll Clubs.

She is a member of the Executive Board of the Flushing Art League, the Doll Collector's Guild of New York (past President), the National League of American Pen Women, and an artist member of the Queens Branch, NLAPW. She was elected to NIADA in 1970.

Jake Jacobson. L to R: posed in costume; doll portrait in costume; in mufti.

"I Cash Clothes Man." Oldtime character from Queens.

"Journey for Peace." President Richard M. Nixon, Chairman Mao of Red China, February, 1972. Group was presented to President Nixon, May, 1972.

Hobo King. Based on 1970 Hobo King, elected on National Hobo Day, Frett, Iowa.

Rose Sullo and her Singing Waiters.

The Doughboy, 1918.

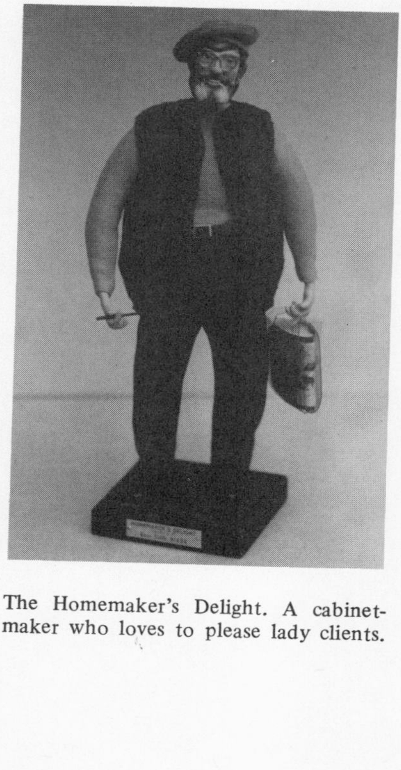

The Homemaker's Delight. A cabinet-maker who loves to please lady clients.

CHAPTER 14

Judith Condon

JUDITH CONDON was born in Boston and had the great good fortune of living many years within sight of the Metropolitan Museum of Fine Arts. As a child she studied drawing and sculpture in Museum classes. Later she studied art at Boston University and in various classes thereafter.

After she was married her mother started collecting old and contemporary dolls and Judy was inspired to start her first two dolls. They were Russian ballet dancers about twenty-two inches tall, made on cloth-covered wire armatures with heads of plastic wood and realistic glass eyes. She was so busy looking after their three children and helping her husband with his business, however, that the dolls were never finished. Her interest in her mother's collection grew along with the collection. One of her special favorites was Magge Head's "Eleanor Roosevelt."

In 1970, Judith and her children moved to Naples, Florida. The children were now old enough to pursue their own interests in rocks, shells, coins, butterflies, and old bicycle parts and their mother was free to go back to dollmaking.

Condon experimented with many media, mostly ceramic clay and porcelain, though she spent some time with plastic wood, papier mache, and wax over papier mache. She finally settled on porcelain and learned to make plastic molds. ("What a drag!" is her comment on this.) She finished the early ballet dancers and went on to other subjects, notably "Ann" and "Gertrude," the Gibson Girls, which she made first in ceramic clay and then repeated in porcelain. The same routine was used in producing a black boy and a fully-jointed court jester.

She is presently working on a series of the children of her Florida area with idealized slender body proportions. They are one-of-a-kind, mostly fully-jointed porcelain, some papier mache, and others wax over porcelain. The experimental ones are Fiberglas and rubber.

Her irrepressible spirit of fun usually comes through in her dolls giving them a vibrant life of their own. This is particularly notable in "Rosey the Witch" who, though witch-y is a rollicking character with a brightly wicked look.

In 1972 Judith Condon was voted into NIADA, met her first artists in dolls at the Omaha convention, and returned home full of enthusiasm and new ideas.

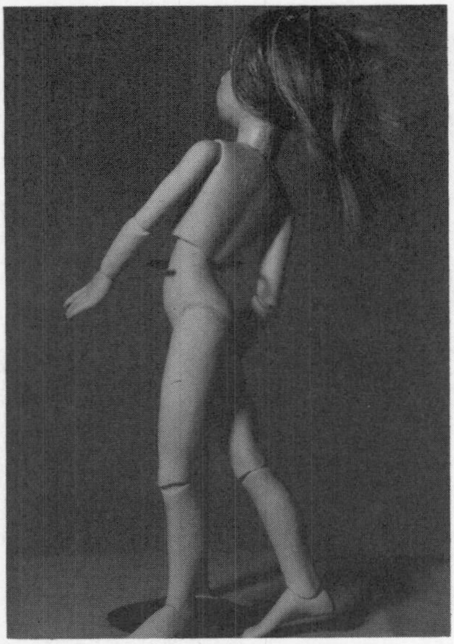

Body Style No. 1. All Condon child bodies are similar.

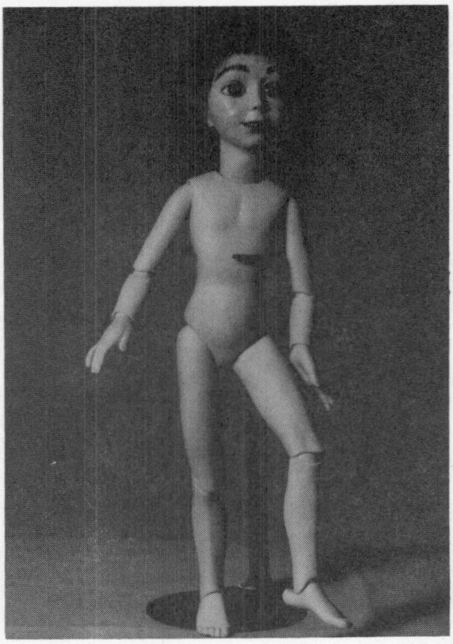

Body Style No. 2.

Hugo. Court jester in various costumes; one Sanford (small).

Louisa. A Gibson Girl with wax-over-porcelain face.

Rosey the Witch.

Little Lena and Leroy with Big Paul.

First dolls, made in 1956. Russian ballet dancers with heads of plastic wood.

Judith Condon with two versions of Michael.

Sanford. Choreographer, with Hilda, Vickie, Kathy, Becky.

CHAPTER 15

Fern Deutsch

IF you had your choice you might easily choose to be born to a mother who was a display artist, that is, if you were intent on creating original dolls. This was the lucky accident which befell Fern Gallagher Deutsch of San Antonio, Texas, and she has made the most of it. She learned the basics of design and construction of display figures by working with her mother, Fannie Pierce Goodwin, who enjoyed great success in the field of department store displays in New York during the 1930s through the 1950s.

Fern Deutsch returned to her home in San Antonio in 1940. After many years of successful work in display in New York, she wished to be near her sons, Albert and James, who were in military school. There she set up her own display studio in partnership with her talented aunt, Besse McGee. They produced seasonal displays, particularly Christmas and Easter items, for department and jewelry stores. Their figures were used for window and interior display and ranged in height from nine inches to six feet. The smaller figures were sold in gift departments and in exclusive shops.

During the 1950s Deutsch added more detail to the features whereupon doll collectors began to show an interest in the figures. Since 1960, her main work has been in dolls, filling commissions for collectors and museums alike. Mrs. Deutsch designed the dolls and modeled heads and hands while Mrs. McGee did the exacting construction and finishing work. Their figures have been widely exhibited in churches and clubs. In 1968, a large exhibit was featured at "Hemisfair," the World's Fair in San Antonio, and in

1969 the Witte Museum in San Antonio staged a special Christmas exhibit of American subjects featuring the twenty-piece Nativity Scene.

Their elaborate nativity scenes have been widely shown for many years. Some were done in hand-sculptured fabric. Later Deutsch dolls have padded fabric or chamois-covered bodies built on sturdy wire armatures that allow them to stand firmly. Heads and hands are made of a special formula of composition covered with kidskin and painted in oil; each face reflects a distinct personality. Mrs. Deutsch and Mrs. McGee make all the clothing and accessories after extensive research so that every piece is historically correct. They also make all the shoes, hats, bags, gloves, parasols, watches, jewelry, and other accessories.

The camels in the nativity scenes are their greatest triumph. The carefully painted kid construction is convincing and lifelike; the camels' faces are solemn and wise. The early nativity scenes, elaborate and colorful, seemed large when the first one was finished in 1961. It included twenty pieces: Mary, Joseph, the Baby Jesus, three kings, two shepherds, three camels, an ox, a donkey, three sheep, two palm trees, a shed, and the jeweled star. The latest one, finished and exhibited in 1973, contains forty-seven pieces! Mary, Joseph, the Baby Jesus, three kings, six shepherds, three camels, twenty sheep, an ox, a donkey, eight palms, the shed, and the jeweled star. The grandeur of the total effect elicits a chorus of ohs and ahs from the crowds of viewers whenever it is put on exhibition.

Fern Deutch was elected to NIADA in 1966.

Boy Fisherman. Early 1900. 12½ inches.

Fern Deutsch and Besse McGee with Nativity Group.

Girl with Doll; Boy with Dog. Late 1800s style.

Carol Singers. Boy with French horn, girl singing, and man with bass. 19-inch adults.

The Fern Deutsch Method of Body Construction

Work steps for frame of fully wired, padded, fabric-covered girl doll, 13½-14 inches tall.

Seven shaped parts

Materials used

1. Florist wire, 18" long, 16 guage
2. Handi-wire, medium guage for securing joints
3. Strong masking tape, ½" or ¾" wide for holding wrap, for assembling frame parts

Steps for Frame assembly

1. Using parts #1 and #2 which are identically shaped pieces, point #1 arm to left and point #2 arm to right.

   Length of arm is approximately 7¼" from corner bend.

   Length of leg is approximately 10" from corner bend.

   Overlap the arm lengths to establish the shoulder width; approximately 2" for girl and 2¼" for boy.

2. Tape the overlapped wires together with strong masking tape (½" or ¾") across the shoulder line.

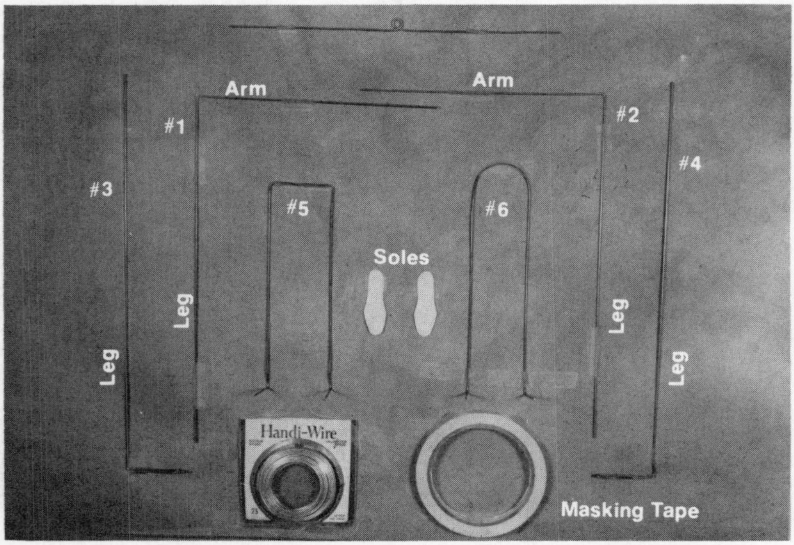

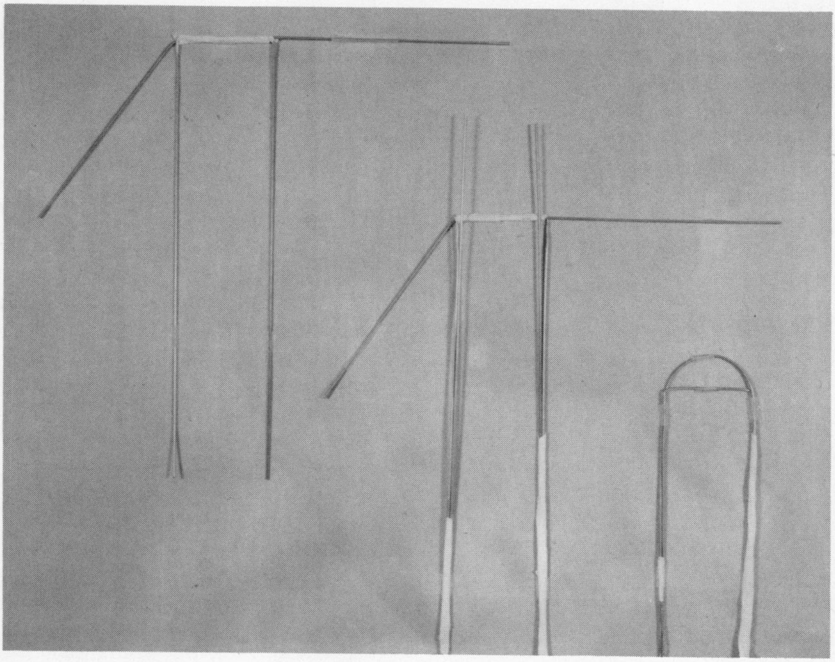

3. Using parts #3 and #4, tape the 12½" leg wires to the right and left legs, with the rounded loop forward so that the loop becomes the fore part of the foot. Tape upward from the floor line to about the hip line. These leg wires will extend above the shoulder approximately 2".
4. Place parts #5 and #6 together with small patches of tape to establish the hip and pelvis width of approximately 2".

   Then tape firmly and smoothly to the legs of step 3, beginning at the floor line, setting the forward wires within the rounded loop to further strengthen the foot structure. Keep all three wires flat to the floor line and hold together with tape.
5. Draw #3 and #4 wires together to form the neck wire. The straight wire which extends to left and right of the center can then be taped firmly along the arm wires. Add smooth layers of tape to all parts until the frame is firm enough to stand alone with minor shifting or adjustments to obtain its balance.

   Add the foot sole cut-outs to the bottom of the feet with strong adhesive. Allow ample time to dry in place.

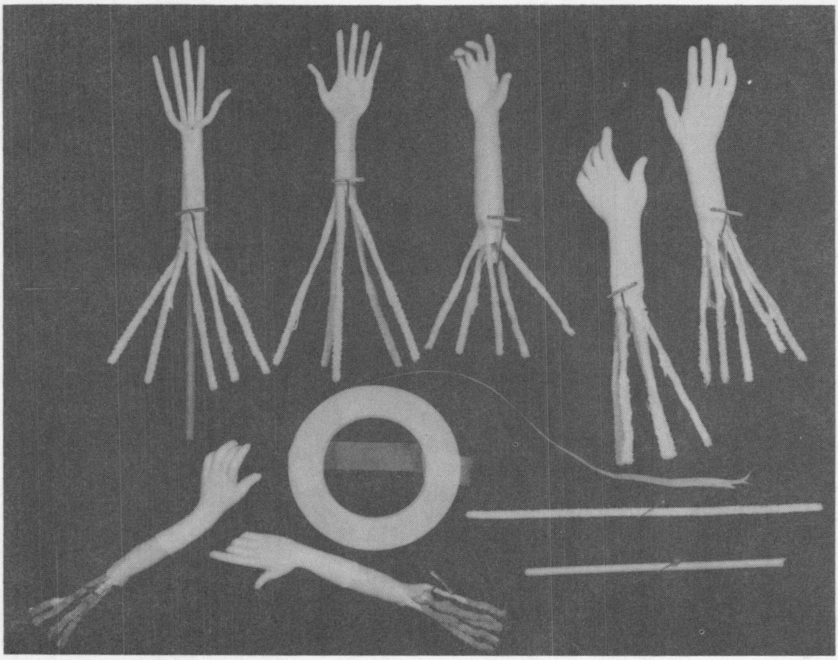

6. Estimate the point of the wrist joints and add the hands by guiding the arm wires into the center opening of the loose hand wires to the point of the wrist joint.

   Gather the end wires of the hand together upward and flat against the arm. Tape firmly as far as they extend along the arm length.

7. Twist a hard wrap of medium guage Handi-wire around all joints of the taped frame, at arms, shoulders, ankles, knees, hips, and elbows. Wire above and below knees and elbows to make posing easier.

8. **Padding the Body**

   Lay on soft tissue paper, or paper napkins to fill out the form. Tape patches will provide a temporary hold until the tissue can be bound to the frame with strong thread; keep the wrapping process of paper and thread in layers–winding, binding, and building the body with additional pieces until the natural shape is achieved.

9. Lay thin layers of smooth cotton over the paper-padded form. Use fine thread to hold lightly in place. Figure is then ready for leg and body cover of stretch jersey.

10. Place the painted head which has a neck opening onto the neck wires. By turning, tipping, or tilting slightly for a natural and pleasing attitude, decide on position. Then remove and coat the inside of head generously with a strong adhesive, replace head on body and gently press the neck to blend and settle into the cotton of the shoulder line.

Hands

Materials

1. Regular size pipe cleaners for 12" to 16" figure; larger pipe cleaners or wired chenille for 18" or over.
2. Floratape stem wrap (Florist supplies) for a smooth, sealed wrapping of fingers and hand.
3. Mod-Podge for first dipping.
4. Liquitex gesso for second and third dips. (Allow overnight drying time between dips.)

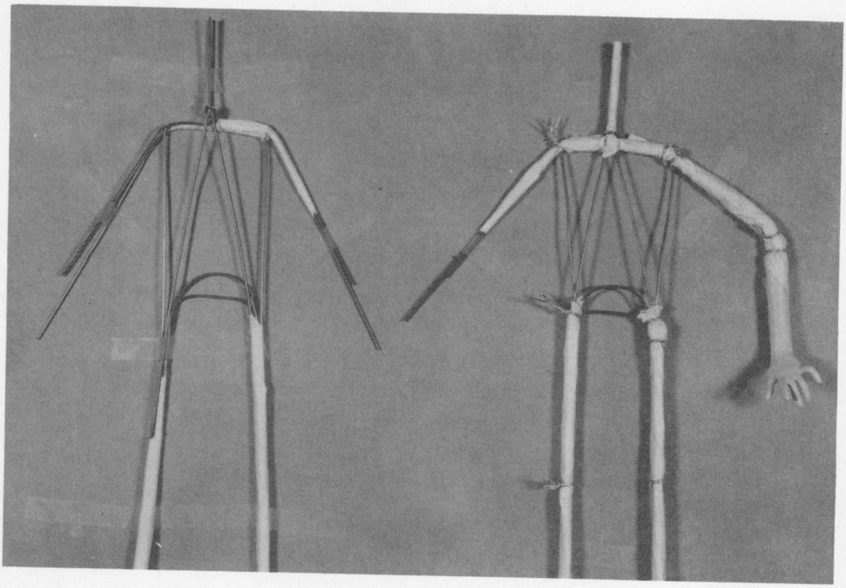

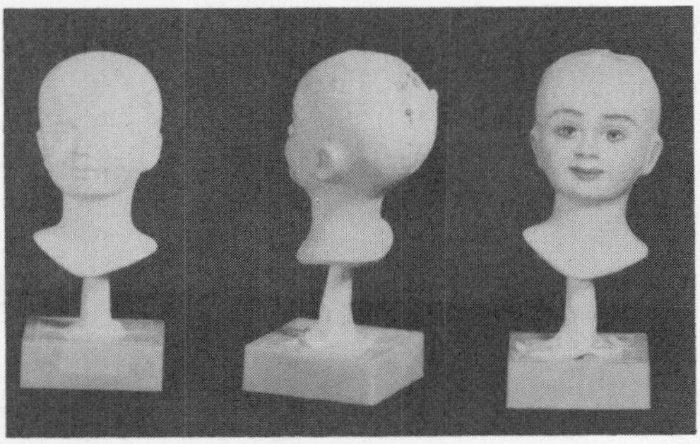

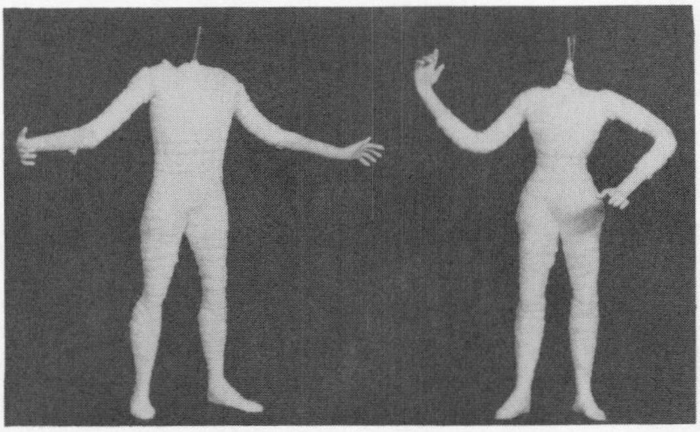

Fingers—10 pieces

1. Wrap with a downward slant from tip of the pipe cleaner about 3" or 3½" using the Floratape, keeping a smooth sealed wrap.
2. Add second wrap in the same manner, beginning slightly below the tip—downward at a slant over the first wrap, keeping smooth. Add about five or six wraps, each slightly lower for a beginning point, downward over other wraps. When the finger seems to be sized to a tapering finger make ten alike.
3. Estimate finger length and palm to wrist. Take three wrapped fingers and attach with Floratape to a small stick, with middle finger to be longer than the other two, with the stick at the wrist joint.
4. Bend thumb wire and little finger wire. Move these together on back side of the stick, little finger to the right, and thumb to the left (reverse for other hand). Wrap well from the wrist on down. This is the palm of the hand.
5. Continue to form the hand with layers of tape, smoothing and sealing together with pressure. Avoid lumps and ridges; closing across the hand at a point of the knuckles.

6. Pose the hands at the wrist and bend the separated fingers into any desired natural position. Remove the small stick with a gentle twist, leaving a center canal to accommodate arm wires.

7. Spread all the pipe cleaner endings so that they will support the dipped hand and serve as a stand to allow the liquid to flow from fingertips downward toward a point beyond the wrist. This is a little wasteful, but insures a smoother surface.

8. Hand is now ready for dips. With fingers down, using a large mouthed jar deep enough for the hand to be submerged in liquid dip, immerse hand to the wrist. Turn back and forth until it is thickly coated, then turn over with fingers up to stand on spread-out wire endings. Allow ample drying time between dips. (Use up to three dips.)

   Hand may be painted or dipped into a hard, quick-dry enamel to furnish a base coat for the final hand painting in permanent oil colors.

9. Tint, shade, and paint in permanent oils to match face complexion.

CHAPTER 16

Pat Robinson

AS a child on a farm along the coast of Maine, Pat Robinson made and dressed dolls using old catalogs and wallpaper sample books for her paper families. Later she raided her grandmother's rag bag and progressed to cloth dolls with "real" dresses. When cloth dolls proved inadequate as fashion manikins, she carved figures of wood to serve her needs.

Her formal art training began at Cass Technical High School in Detroit where she studied costume illustration and fashion design, expanding her grasp of these subjects with much actual work in the field. Her job always had art-related duties, such as the one in a decorative repair studio where she remodeled dress manikins with plaster and airbrush. Another job as a cake decorator provided an opportunity to paint portraits on cakes with sugar and coloring.

Her marriage to Mel Robinson and the births of their three children caused a long interruption in her art career. When the children were all in school Pat returned to work on dolls, built up her antique doll collection to hugh proportions, joined the Detroit Collectors' Club, and went to work on original dolls of her own.

She took two dolls to the national convention of the United Federation of Doll Clubs in 1964 and won a third prize. "I figured the dolls were too small, so the following year I entered three large ones and won three first prices," she says.

At first she worked with wood and ceramic clays, then experimented with wax, papier mache, cloth, and even apple heads, settling finally on porcelain, because of the molded replicas possible in this fine material. At succeeding national conventions she won fifteen more ribbons, most of them blue, and saw her dolls widely displayed and featured. During the 1970 UFDC convention in Detroit, the Detroit Historical Museum staged a show of her portrait figures and her "Theresa Tonty," representing the first white child born in Detroit (1702), appeared on the cover of the Convention Souvenir Book. In May, 1972, her Engelbert Humperdinck portrait doll appeared on the cover of *Doll News,* the UFDC quarterly.

Pat Robinson has made many portrait dolls, some of them quite large. Included are the Kennedys, Abraham Lincoln, Mona Lisa, Clark Gable, Dean Martin, Engelbert Humperdinck, Tom Jones, her daughter Marcia, and a self-portrait. She now creates each figure entirely of porcelain with moving joints, using the fifteen to eighteen inch size. All are resculptured and individualized.

She was elected to NIADA in 1967.

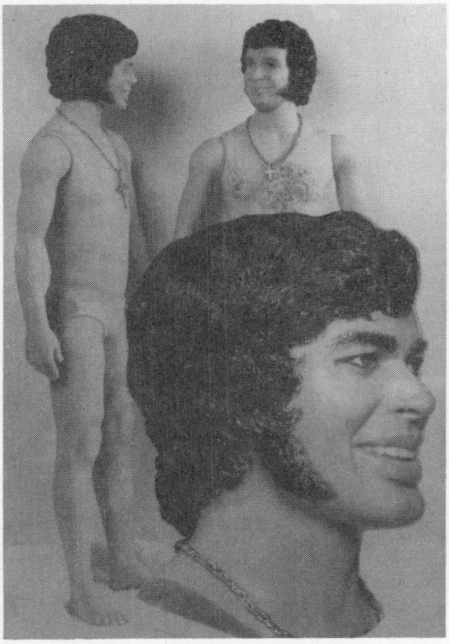

Engelbert Humperdinck and Tom Jones. Singers; Engelbert close-up.

Self-portrait.

Clark Gable.

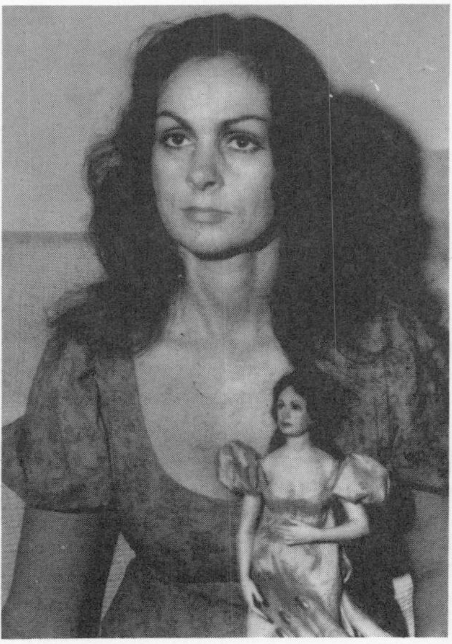

Pat Robinson with self-portrait doll.

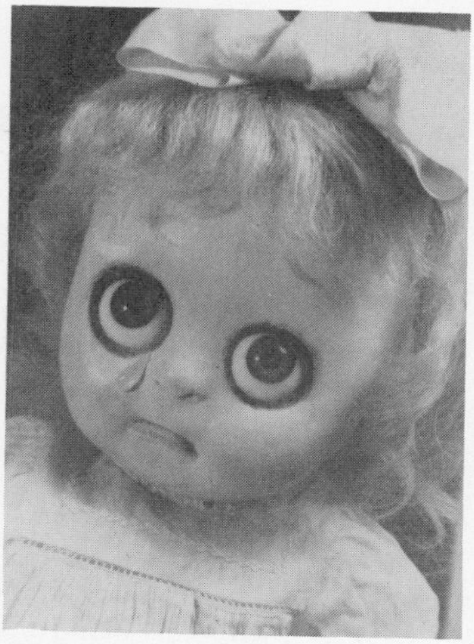

Getsya. Two-faced hand-carved wood. (Tearful)

Jack and Jackie. President and Mrs. John F. Kennedy.

CHAPTER 17

Mirren Barrie

WHEN Mirren Barrie's daughter went to Denmark to meet her fiance's family, his mother said, "I have read, in one of your magazines, of an American artist who makes fabric dolls like the ones you tell me your mother makes. Could your mother be that artist?" Mirren's daughter had never heard of the article; however, in 1972, when the mother-in-law met Mirren she exclaimed, "Yes, you are the artist in the photograph I saw!" Alas, Mirren Barrie has never been able to obtain a copy of that feature story but she knows her work has been noticed far afield.

She was born in the ancient Royal Burgh of Rutherglen, Scotland, which received its charter first from King David and again from Robert the Bruce in the thirteenth century. It was a thriving town when Glasgow, six miles away, was only a huddle of mud huts. From age twelve Mirren studied general subjects and art at the Glasgow High School for Girls. Further art studies were impossible because of her father's business reverses so she learned shorthand and typing and went to work. She escaped office work by studying all sorts of crafts at night on her own.

Marriage, the births of two daughters, and a sojourn in Hampshire, England, intervened before the family returned to Scotland and Mirren resumed her interest in crafts. As an active member of the Townswomen's Guild she taught many craft classes, giving exhibitions and demonstrations. When the Guild offered a high-level course in embroidery she enrolled. After three years of study culminating in a three-day examination she reluctantly quit to go to America, her husband having been transferred to the Detroit office of his company.

Years earlier in Scotland she had begun making soft toys for fun. As her knowledge of needlework had grown and her skill improved the toys she made became more detailed. Eventually she decided she must stop giving them away and make something to sell. The opportunity came from the Scottish Craft Centre which wanted quality dolls representing Scottish women in occupational costumes.

Knowing nothing of these things Barrie spent long hours in concentrated research at the Mitchell Library in Glasgow. The dolls proved a great success and she supplied the Centre for two seasons. Then for a British Craft Exhibition she chose Rob Roy MacGregor, a Scottish "Robin Hood" who was active in the early eighteenth century when English forces occupied forts in Scotland.

When no MacGregor tartan in scale for a fifteen-inch doll could be found, Barrie wove a length of Rob Roy's own tartan. Her husband Tod, one of whose hobbies is silver work, crafted the sword, dirk, and targe, or shield. Of the twenty thousand items submitted, only two hundred were displayed at Olympia, London, and Rob Roy was the only doll chosen to make his bow before royalty. He has since taken first place wherever he has been shown.

Mirren gave up dolls for seven years and then, through the International Institute in Detroit, she received an order for two dolls, a Romanian and a Ukrainian. Her research was complicated by the fact that the only book on Romanian costume was in French. With the aid of a dictionary she translated the entire book and made the dolls all the while delighting in their purpose for they were to be a nativity gift for a little girl with Romanian and Ukrainian grandmothers.

Barrie continued to make ethnic dolls based on meticulous research and developed her present method of construction which begins with a wire armature without arms. She checks for balance at every stage of construction because her dolls are free-standing. Legs and arms are made of felt, hand-stitched and fitted over the padded leg and arm wires. Both fingers and thumbs of the mitten hands are wired with pliable wire so they may hold tools or be positioned naturally.

Torsos and heads on the twelve-inch dolls are layers of cotton, butter muslin, and fine paper soaked in glue, applied over a sculptured form made of low-fired clay. The laminated material is pressed into the desired contours and allowed to dry for about twenty-four hours. Since temperature and humidity vary greatly, wrinkles sometimes form in exactly the right places. If the desired effect is not obtained, the piece is discarded and the process repeated. Features are painted with inks or acrylics and the wig is then attached.

In Mary, Queen of Scots, silk chiffon was used for a more elegant look. When Mary's aquiline nose kept breaking off under the silk mask Barrie was tempted to abandon the Stuart profile entirely but persisted until the problem was solved.

Each Barrie doll is signed and numbered on the back as is the small descriptive card accompanying each doll. More important is the warm friendly personality of the artist expressed in the humor or character of the doll.

In 1973, the Barries retired to a cottage overlooking a wooded Vermont valley where they are busily creating dolls. Mirren Barrie was elected to NIADA in 1970.

Mirren Barrie and Ten of Her People Figures.

Mistress Bronwen and husband, Merchant Morgan. 1800, Welsh.

Mhairi Robertson. The Scottish peat-gatherer.

CHAPTER 18

Sharon Johnson

WITH a father who is an artist and a mother who operates a doll shop Sharon Johnson had an early start toward becoming a doll artist. She began by painting portraits in oil with the help of her father and soon found her interest so great that she spent a year studying art. Marriage and three small children brought new interests, then one day her mother suggested she try to model a doll. Pulling out her well-read copy of Elizabeth Andrews Fisher's *Doll Stuff* (1959 Middletown, Connecticut) she made up a batch of sawdust and wallpaper paste dough and modeled a doll. The man which emerged after several hours' concentrated effort looked like a Kentucky colonel and because her father is from Kentucky she immediately gained a sympathetic and admiring audience.

Sharon was sure then that dolls were what she wanted to make. This first one was crude, however, and she knew she must have a better material. There followed a feverish research period in which she visited all the nearby libraries, art schools, and art shops; she even called the more distant ones to learn more about materials. Nowhere could she find help on dolls, but she was able to select a self-hardening clay as her material.

Sharon was lucky. Her mother took the best modeled heads, hands, and feet, made cloth bodies, assembled the dolls, and costumed them, while Sharon went on making heads. Nearly two years later a customer of her mother's mentioned that Magge Head was in Indiana only an hour's drive away and regularly gave classes in modeling and mold making. Magge Head was interested in Sharon Johnson's work and accepted her for the fall modeling class which was a week long.

Everyone worked from nine to nine and crammed every bit of information and practice possible into each day. Sharon was anxious to make a portrait doll and Magge arranged for "Grandma" Plankenhorn, who prepared meals for the class members, to pose for her. The resulting "Lady Margaret" doll, dressed in a turn-of-the-century red wool costume, ranks with Johnson's best work.

Magge Head's husband, Keith Kane, made a mold of the Lady Margaret head and when Sharon saw her work, reproduced in porcelain she knew she wanted to work in this marvelous medium. Her mother offered her a partnership in her Mother-Daughter Doll House and financed preparations for the reproduction of Sharon's dolls in porcelain. Sharon's mother, Gladys Pergram, still does the bodies and the costuming. Many of us envy Sharon this working partnership.

Her first commissioned portrait doll was of Jean Thomas known as the "Traipsin' Woman" of Ashland, Kentucky, and an early collector of folksongs in the Kentucky hills. Many other commissioned portraits have followed. Johnson alternates these with original groups such as the "Playmates of the Past" series which will cover a hundred years of American children. She has also done a series on religious sects of her area; Ohio has had settlements of Dunkards, or River Brethren, Amish, Mennonites, Quakers, and Shakers. Each set of these dolls is limited to twelve copies.

Sharon Johnson was elected to NIADA in 1967. She lives in Germantown, Ohio.

"Playmates of the Past." L to R: Gladys and Christine; Young Will and Ruby Mae; Dimple and Derek.

Lady Margaret. 20 inches.

Priscilla.

Sharon Johnson and Her Mother, Gladys Pergram, at Doll Show.

CHAPTER 19

Eunice Tuttle

EUNICE TUTTLE has always loved tiny things and dolls, so it was not surprising that at age nine she was making paper dolls with fountain pen, writing paper, and scissors. What was surprising was that by using her father's scale rule she made them accurately scaled at one-quarter inch to the foot. As her collection grew to include whole families she no longer waited eagerly for the *Ladies Home Journal* to appear with its doll families.

When her doll families outgrew their paper box she decided she could make furniture for them herself. She devoted an entire summer to the creation of beds, tables, chairs, a crib with bars, a baby carriage, and a piano using the same materials plus a little paste. Later she acquired a series of dollhouse dolls which she dressed. Eventually she wanted to make the dolls as well as the costumes; she whittled wooden dolls and sewed rag ones, then dressed them as she pleased. Usually she gave them to the first person who asked for them because, once finished, a doll ceased to interest her. She was on an experimental search and thought only of the next doll which would be better and different. She says she felt 'entitled' to one doll-creating spree a year for some time.

Eunice Tuttle was born in Brooklyn and graduated from the Pratt Institute course in general art, applied design, and crafts. After three years as an industrial designer in textiles, she returned to Pratt for a year of work which led to a certificate in teacher education. She then taught art in public schools for many years.

She continued to take courses, including jewelry making and enameling, marionette making with Tony Sarg, and two years of ceramics with Amy Voorhees of Inwood Potteries in New York City. She designed and constructed scenery for several productions of the Gilbert and Sullivan Society of White Plains. She developed a line of dollhouse-size porcelain dolls and began selling them in 1960. In 1963 she took an early retirement in order to devote herself to dollmaking. Later with her sister she moved to Lakewood, New Jersey, her present home.

Recent Tuttle dolls are all dollhouse-size children scaled one inch to the foot. They represent either modern boys and girls, both black and white, or children from famous paintings such as those of Renoir, Goya, and Velasquez. They range in size from babies of two and one-fourth inches to the eight-year-olds which measure four and one-half inches. Miss Tuttle's precise craftsmanship lends great elegance to her miniatures.

After experimenting with various types of clay, she now uses a very fine grade of pink porcelain slip which produces a beautiful smooth bisque. All the clothing is carefully researched and she makes all patterns and clothing as well as the tiny accessories required.

Incised in the porcelain on the back of each doll is the doll's name, the number and date of firing, and the artist's name. She makes molds from her own models and each doll is individually trimmed and finished so as to have its own distinct personality. Instead of issuing a catalog and taking orders for dolls as she used to do, she now finds it more creative and interesting to be constantly making new dolls.

Eunice Tuttle's twin interests, dolls and teaching, were admirably served by a special project completed late in her teaching career. She designed, constructed, and furnished a dollhouse to be used in teaching perspective drawing to seventh-graders. Elizabeth Andrews Fisher showed this dollhouse in her book, *Miniature Stuff* (1964) and it has been exhibited and discussed before many school, doll club, and church groups. She was elected to NIADA in 1968.

Eunice Tuttle's process of dollmaking has been the subject of many lectures. An outline of her methods is included in this account.

Thomas. Five-year-old, 4 inches. Katie. Five-year-old, 4 inches. From Kate Greenaway illustrations.

Tammie. Three-year-old, 3½ inches. Angel Baby. Four-month-old, 2¼ inches.

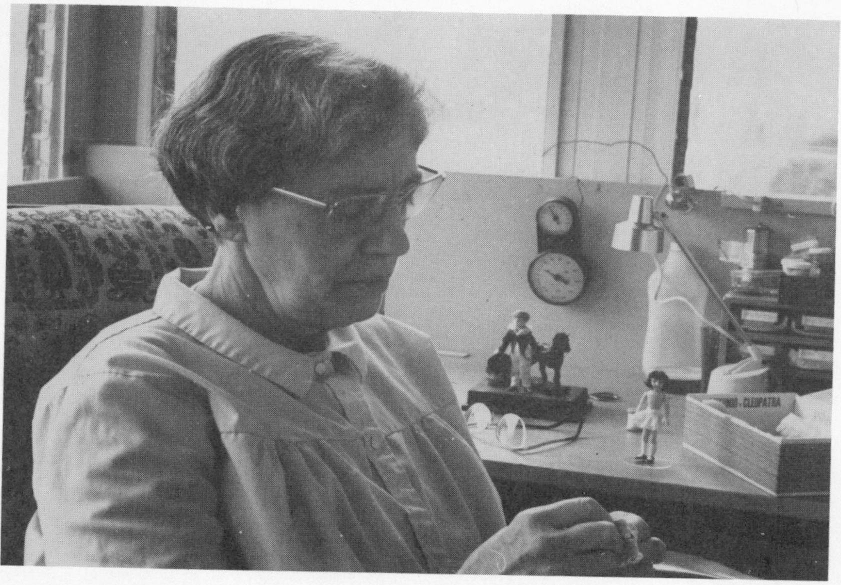

Eunice Tuttle at Work. On work bench is Pepito Costa y Bonells, five-year-old, 4 inches. Colette, five-year-old, 4 inches.

Infanta Margarita Maria. Five-year-old, 4 inches. From the painting "Los Meninas."

Don Manuel Osorio. Five-year-old, 4 inches. From the Goya painting.

Girl with a Water Can. Five year-old, 4 inches. From the Renoir painting.

Liz. Three-year-old, 3½ inches.

Two Charpentier Children. Three-year-old, 3½ inches; four-year-old, 4 inches. From the painting by Renoir.

Mme. Bergeret.

Infanta Margarita Maria. Three-year-old, 3½ inches. From the painting by Velasquez.

MAKING A PORCELAIN DOLL
according to Eunice P. Tuttle

I. MAKING THE ORIGINAL MODEL

Influence–Velasquez and Renoir prints of children

Reference–Scrapbook of Velasquez Infantas

Exact-size drawings of Velasquez Infantas for model with regard to proportion of figure and shrinkage of clay when fired–12% in her clay.

Tools and Materials:

- Modeling clay–Plasticene or other non-hardening clay
- Modeling tool–scraper–razor blade

II. PLASTER CASTING THE MODEL–STEP #1

Tools and Materials:

- Spoon and mixing bowl
- Measured plaster and measured water
- Old brush (#7) for use in plaster
- Round-end wooden tool for "keying"
- Petroleum jelly and brush for greasing box and plaster–*not* model
- Mask (if allergic to dust)
- Paper toweling for cleanup–*(plaster will clog drains)*
- Cardboard boxes–both sections greased inside
- Wires for supporting model in such a way that the back section is deeper in the plaster than is the front.

Process:

- To avoid waste, figure volume of boxes for amount of plaster formula: .543 oz. plaster and ½ cup of water to 1 cu. in.
- Grease box–*not* model–inside
- Mix plaster–sprinkle plaster on water in bowl until water will absorb no more plaster–allow to stand for two minutes and then stir carefully to avoid bubbles forming.
- Pour into lower part of box when the mixture begins to thicken.
- Fill box *almost* full–allow for volume model will displace.
- Place model in plaster so that the wires rest on the top edges of the box–this holds the model in place until the plaster sets.
- Pull out the wires when the plaster has set (no longer takes a fingerprint) and the model is firmly encased in plaster at the required level.
- Smooth out with palette knife if the wires leave a groove.
- Make "keys" (round indentations in plaster) for second pouring which will be the front of the doll.
- Remove (tear off) the cardboard box after thirty minutes.
- Allow to dry and cool for at least an hour (plaster heats as chemical action sets in).

III. PLASTER CASTING–STEP #2

- Put cardboard collar–twice as high as lower cast–around the cast using a rubber band to hold it in place.
- Grease upper surface of lower cast and inside of box–*not the model.*
- Mix plaster as before.
- Brush plaster around edges of model and features–eyes, nose,

and edges.

Pour in remaining plaster to fill up box.

Allow to set; remove collar from box.

Mark name and date on front and back of cast.

Separate after two hours; insert razor blade at joint mark and tap lightly. Thorough greasing makes for easy separation.

Remove model from cast; it will probably not come out in one piece.

Allow cast to dry four or five days before casting with slip.

Saw back section of cast in half the long way for ease of removal where there are undercuts.

This is for the body and head sections of the model. Use the same method for hands and feet using smaller boxes; it is not necessary to cut these sections as was done with the back of the body-head piece.

IV. POURING PORCELAIN SLIP IN THE CAST

Clay:

Bell's White Orchid Porcelain Slip–Dark Pink Slip is a mixture of clay and a deflocculant (liquifying agent) and comes ready to use.

Tools:

Small brush for filling in features first.

Spoon to finish filling with slip.

Palette knife for trimming clay from top of cast.

Procedure:

Front and back of cast, open side up on table, hold two bottom pieces together with elastic band while pouring.

Brush in slip carefully to avoid bubble formation around features.

Fill in rest of cavity with spoonfuls of slip.

Allow to set three to five minutes.

Pour out excess clay–a skin of clay will have adhered to the plaster–with arms and legs allow clay to fill cast completely as these are solid while head-body section is hollow.

Trim top edges carefully, should be flush with top of cast. The thickness of piece will now be apparent–about 1/8"–do not try to save these trimmings.

Brush slip on the trimmed edges and put them back together; slip serves as glue.

Set aside for fifteen minutes.

Carefully open the cast. First remove the elastic band on the bottom piece. Take back sections off separately leaving face part in the cast; the plaster has repelled the slip by this time and as the cast is lifted away the duplicate of the original model is left. Handle with care as the clay is still quite damp.

It is at this point that any changes in features or hand positions should be made, while the clay is damp–otherwise keep in a "damp box" until such time as this can be done. Make arm and leg openings while clay is wet. Remember to allow for shrinkage of openings. Dry pieces slowly on a "bat"–*no heat.*

V. TRIMMING THE CAST PIECES

Tools:

Stencil knife—small—not sharp
Brushes for smoothing
Finger scraper (small pointed tool)
Brush for dusting
Piece of nylon stocking for final polish
A tortillion (paper)
A mask—*most important of all*—porcelain clay is toxic when inhaled.

Procedure:

Trim away all excess clay or rough places—I find this the best time to trim seams although some authorities frown on this.
Clean up details—eyes, nose, mouth, ears, and fingers—with scraper.
Smooth by rubbing gently with nylon stocking.
Use tortillion to smooth hard-to-reach details—ears, eyes, etc.
Incise on back of body—name of doll, date, your name, and register mark.

VI. FIRING THE CAST PIECES

The Kiln—Test Kiln—AMACO—rewired with Kanthal wire to fire to 2400 degrees.

Procedure:

Firing #1—Place the trimmed pieces on a kiln-shelf which has been well coated, on top, with high-fire kiln-wash—no stilts —pieces must *not* touch each other.
Place Cone 5 (about 2300 degrees) just inside the peep-hole where it can be seen when peep-hole is opened.
Turn on *all controls*—low, medium, and high—leave door open a bit for thirty to forty minutes.
Shut door tight and leave same heat on for about an hour or until cone bends.
Shut off power and leave kiln unopened for five hours.
Remove pieces when cool and polish with rubber scrubber.
Firing #2—Again place the pieces in kiln in same fashion.
Place Cone #6 (2400 degrees) in position.
Fire in same way but leave heat on for one and one-half hours after the door is closed or until cone melts.
Allow to cool six hours.
Fired doll is now ready for assembling—no more polishing.

VII. ASSEMBLY – PAINTING – WIGGING

Attaching tools:

Cutting and twisting pliars (long nose).
Brass wire to fit arm and leg openings.
Paste—all-purpose white glue.

Paints:

Watercolors for eyes—#00000 brush—clear nail polish.
Flopaque, coral, red, and thinner for cheeks and lips.
Dekall, white and black, for shoes and socks.

Wigging:

Rayon braid or shoelaces
Pink cotton material for scalp (very fine)
Water and stiff "oil brush" for setting

The doll is now ready for dressing; use fine materials and thread.

CHAPTER 20

Irma Park

SOME artists seem to have been born to create original dolls and others have tried everything else first and then 'landed' in the doll field. Of the latter group Irma Park seems to take first prize. One day in the mid-thirties she and her mother arrived in Los Angeles alone and broke—so much so that Irma remembers wanting to write a letter and not daring to spend the two cents for a stamp. Irma found work as a bookkeeper at sixteen dollars a week and, somehow, by 1939 they had saved enough to buy out two small gift stocks and set up a little gift shop with her mother in charge.

Irma confesses that in those years she was driven by a strong need for a recognized success, something of her own. In her mind she was at the foot of a long stairway leading up a hill, with a hammock under a shade tree at the top. With the gift shop as an outlet, she tried making just about everything in her after-work hours: hobbies, puzzles, pattern books, inventions, a steak cuber, a weed digger, a doll with movable expressions (before pliable vinyl), newspaper pieces from philosophic sayings, and modeled figures for ads or magazine covers. But none of these carried her up that stairway.

In the early forties she needed a jointed figure to pose for a photograph and from a thrift shop she purchesed a ball-jointed, bisque-headed doll. She was unable to pose the doll properly so it was placed in the shop and sold. This led to buying more old dolls, not to sell but to keep. Irma's interest in dolls led her to attempt making one of her own using buckram pressed into molds. She was not entirely pleased with the resulting twelve-inch doll.

Her mother, who had painted in oil since she was thirteen, made gift items for the shop. Among them were rose-trimmed trays of composition which in 1944 caught the eye of a salesman who brought her some ceramic clay. Irma and her mother bought a kiln, set it up in the shop, and Irma quit her job to learn ceramic modeling and casting. They went into production and by 1945 were so successful they were able to buy a 1942 Packard and a house. They soon added a workroom which housed a small mass-production operation with outlets all over the country. Their line, called "Lenora Ceramics," included hand-crimped and molded bowls, trays, baskets, and vases, hand-decorated with roses, stems, and buds. Many people tried vainly to copy her mother's roses, the detail which accounted for the great success of their ceramic ware. Her mother had achieved a personal success, but Irma's was yet to come.

Success meant very hard work for six years, during which Irma and her mother labored day and night. They took off one afternoon a week to go "junking," often returning with the Packard full of old dolls, mostly German bisques, for the museum they hoped one day to have. In need of a rest by 1951, they sold the house and equipment and moved to a rural area. Still thinking of the museum, Irma started a set of six and one-half inch dolls representing kings and queens and completed fifty-one of them.

Her mother became an invalid in 1961 and remained so until her death nine years later. Irma had been holding a job for several years and with her mother an invalid she had to quit and try to find work to do at home. Since dolls were her main interest, she tried dollmaking. First came character dolls with wired cloth bodies and a wax coating over a cornstarch formula for the head, arms, and feet. "Peddler Grannie" was the only one perfected beyond the sample stage and was later made in wax over composition.

In 1963 she found an advertisement in Kimport's *Doll Talk* for Dorothy Hesner's one-inch "Minnie Prue" and wondered if she, too, could make tiny dolls. After months of trial and-error, she sent "Notion Grannie" and a few other two and three-fourths inch figures to Kimport. Notion Grannie proved a great success and other characters soon followed, among them Mary, Queen of Scots, Elizabeth I, Joan of Arc, and some clowns.

By 1966 she had turned to children as subjects, attempting still smaller ones, some only one and five-eighths inches and one and seven-eighths inches tall. She says they were not too difficult; they just took time. Achieving a slender, graceful body only one-fourth to one-inch tall was a problem. Another challenge was dressing these tiny dolls without a bulky look. This meant draping and re-draping the fabric. Irma uses a magnifying glass for some of her work.

She says, "I devote all time possible to dolls in the daytime and at night carry the doll work to bed. I turn on the TV and work until eleven or so. Sometimes I find myself dozing with a doll in one hand and needle and thread in the other. As to how they are made, it would be almost impossible to say. A good friend once said they are made with love and maybe that gives me the patience. As I never had any children of my own the little dolls in a way are bits of me to be around awhile after I am gone."

Until 1973 heads, arms, and legs were made of composition and coated with wax, then Irma changed to china-painted porcelain under the wax. On dolls measuring one inch or smaller the hair is painted; larger dolls have combed yarn wigs. Bodies of most are of wire with cotton covering. Depending on the size, there are different ways of assembling a doll and dressing it. Each size presents its own problems. With one it may be in the dressing; with another difficulty may arise with the painting of the features. On one particular one-inch baby the mouth was painted and wiped off seven times before Irma Park was satisfied.

Irma writes, "My big day arrived on August 7, 1969, when I was elected to NIADA. As for that hammock, there is satisfaction in having it in sight, but less time and desire than ever to make use of it." Irma Park has proof that she keeps hard at work, for her second Packard, new in 1949, has less than thirty thousand miles on it!

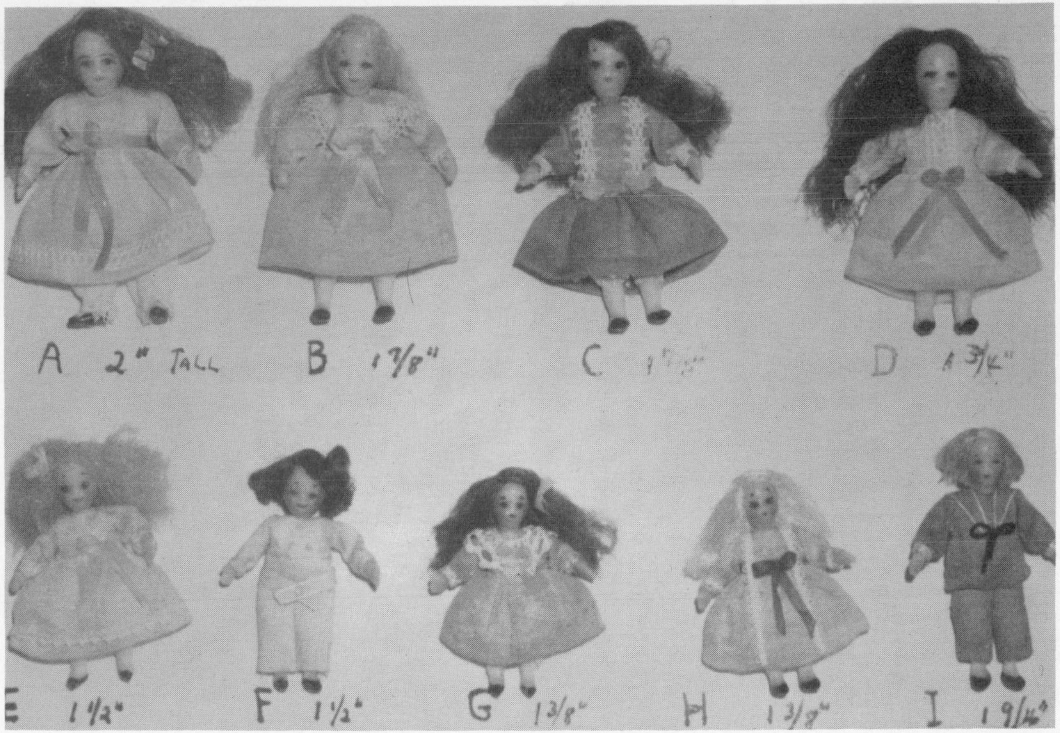

Doll's Dolls. 1-3/16 to 2 inches.

Miniatures. ¼ to 2 inches.

CHAPTER 21

Bernard Ravca

DENIED a medical education by his father's untimely death, young Bernard Ravca took a job painting silk scarfs, shawls, and dolls' faces in a studio near Paris. It angered him that the dolls must all look alike with the same set "pretty" look, so when he was asked to make a doll representing Marguerite, from "Faust," he tried to make her a real personality. He received so much praise for the doll that he opened his own studio, determined to make dolls as different from each other as real people.

A *faux pas* at a fashionable dinner furthered his career remarkably. Absently, he rolled his spilled bread crumbs into a little old face and his dinner partner exclaimed, "But you should do that for a living!" Thus came the inspiration for his prize-winning "Breadcrumb Couple," still his most widely known dolls.

Breadcrumbs have limited possibilities so he searched for a second medium which he developed over a long period. Needle-sculptured cotton with a silk stocking "skin" was used for the head and the body was cotton-stuffed over a wire armature. One day an English lord appeared at his studio to order a pair of French peasant dolls as a gift for his wife. The dolls so pleased the Englishman that he told all his friends and M. Ravca was soon deluged with orders and favorable publicity.

At official request he made fifty representative French dolls for the suite occupied by the young Queen Elizabeth II and Prince Philip in the Quai D'Orsay Palace in Paris during their visit to President LeBrun in July 1938. The Queen expressed her delight in the dolls in a personal letter written to M. Ravca after her return to London.

His work had been winning prizes throughout Europe when at the 1937 Paris Exposition his dolls won a gold medal in the international competition. This distinction led the French Government to send him to New York in 1939 with an exhibition of his dolls for the French Pavilion at the World's Fair. While he was in the United States, France fell to the Nazis and he lost to Germany everything he owned but the doll collection brought over for the Fair. Establishing headquarters in New York, he toured the country giving lectures and exhibitions for the Free French War Relief.

In his early days of dollmaking, Ravca had accumulated many books of national costume and had supplemented this material whenever possible by field research. Cranking up his dilapidated car, Lena, and stowing in Frederick, his handsome black cat, he had bumped through the provinces of France, living with his peasant friends and picking up bits of costume lore and native customs. For instance, he had learned that in Brittany a woman indicates her wealth by the amount of velvet on her Sunday dress.

He soon found his favorite subjects were old people whose wrinkles and character lines could be cleverly suggested in his sculptured cotton faces. Carefully he manipulated his simple materials to make them carry his messages, and just as carefully he spent much time observing faces and storing the impressions in his memory for future use. Some mouths have laugh lines, some sad ones; some cheeks are young and firm, others flabby and old-looking. There are smooth hands and gnarled ones; stooped shoulders and straight; all spell out the wide variety to be seen in people.

Ravca became a sculptor in cotton, for his heads are made entirely of cotton. He stitches here and there to achieve the contours and deep lines, stretches a silk stocking over the head, then paints the coloring and features on the face. Eight hours are required to complete a head. American silk hose are used because they are finer and produce a better effect. Spun wool is used for soft white hair. He also continued to make his famous breadcrumb dolls as long as real French bread, the only kind he likes to work with, was available.

In the States, Ravca repeated his research journeys, visiting eighteen Indian tribes and other groups to obtain first-hand impressions of their appearance and customs. He has created many

American figures, both historical and contemporary, and has shown his doll exhibitions widely in this country.

Bernard Ravca says of his work, "Through the years I had mostly concentrated on the heads and hands while the clothing and most of the bodies were constructed under my supervision by a bevy of ladies, predominantly Tsarist refugees, in my atelier."

The Ravca exhibit in recent years has numbered two thousand dolls, with never two the same. Ravca dolls are easily recognized by experienced doll collectors. Because of the extent of their production, there is no catalog of the Ravca dolls. Suffice to say they consist of old people of various countries in a variety of occupations and poses: French and other provincial and historical European characters, American Indians of eighteen different tribes, ballet dancers, American regional and historical figures, literary figures, actors and actresses, and probably others. His own collection is still large and varied. Bernard Ravca was elected to NIADA in 1968.

Bernard Ravca with three life-size dolls and many of his smaller models.

American Grandmother. 1900.

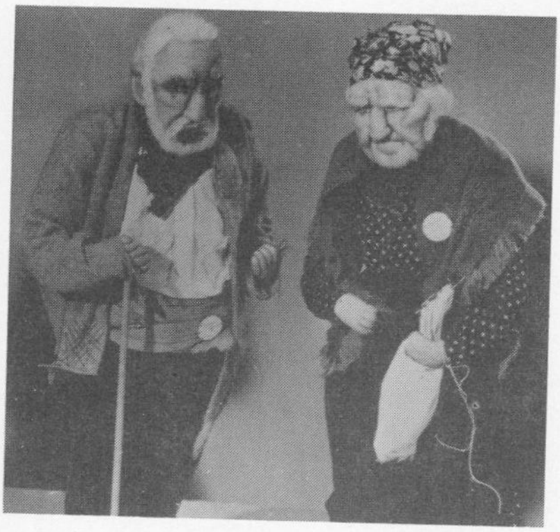

These Parisian Beggers have won eight medals and first prizes.

French Peasants From Various Provinces.

French Bourgeois Couple, the Famous "Breadcrumb Dolls."

More French Peasants.

CHAPTER 22

Frances Diecks Ravca

ALTHOUGH Frances Diecks of Cohoes, New York, made many dolls in her early years, it was not until she had bullied her parents into sending her to the New York School of Fine Arts that she turned to dolls as her medium. The impetus came during a summer spent with friends of Schenectady at the Mohawk Drama Festival, headed by Mr. and Mrs. Charles Coburn. Her delight in meeting famous actresses such as Cornelia Otis Skinner, Bebe Daniels, Sally Eilers, Eugenie Leontovitch, Beulah Bondi, Margaret Anglin, and others brought on the question, "Why not make dolls of these actresses and actors in the costumes of their leading roles?"

Using her training in costume design and sculpture, she set out to do just that. She chose needle-sculptured fabric as a medium, with an individually molded head based on fabric. She made many such figures, pleasing both the subjects and the art and gift shops where her agent introduced the dolls.

Back in New York, with an entre to the theatre, she was invited backstage by Helen Hayes, who was then playing "Victoria Regina." She was allowed to study the actress's costumes and the doll which resulted was enthusiastically received by Miss Hayes. Frances went on to meet and interpret such figures as Mary Margaret McBride, an early radio figure, and some members of the London D'Oyly Carte Opera Company, then playing in New York. The popularity of her figures caused an avalanche of orders and her dolls were sold by finer gift shops throughout the country.

Besides portraits of stage figures, Frances Diecks made a series of ballerinas, inspired by such *premiere danseuses* as

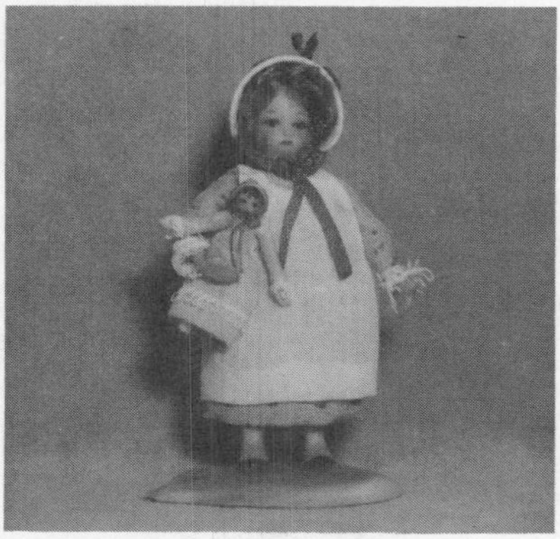

Katie. 2 inches.

Henry III of France and Louise. 6½ inches. ca. 1581.

"First Love". 2 inches.

"Arms Full". 1-7/8 inches.

Peddler Grannie. 11½ inches.

Irma Park (R) with Jane Withers who calls herself Irma's Number One Fan.

Markova, Danilova, and Pavlova in graceful arabesques, pirouettes, entrechats, cabrioles, and glissades. Later an entire exhibition of her ballet figures was widely shown.

Her latest and perhaps favorite doll is "Easter Sunday," a little Black girl taken from life as she dressed for the Easter Parade in New York City.

While visiting an art school classmate in New York, a postcard was forwarded to her from a Parisian dollmaker who had heard of her dolls and wished to meet her when he visited New York. By this time he had arrived and she was persuaded by her friend to go to his studio for an interview. Her friend, a young matron, felt she would be an adequate chaperon and went so far as to taste the wine proferred by M. Bernard Ravca when they were seated in his studio. The wine seemed safe enough and the interview was so enjoyable that the two doll artists corresponded throughout the year of Ravca's American travel with his dolls. They were married in Minneapolis on Thanksgiving Day, 1943, and have since that time worked together on dolls, exhibitions, and the display groups which they have rented to clients for special exhibits throughout the years. The Ravcas no longer travel long distances to give lectures and exhibitions. They live in Jeffersonville, New York, where, as Mr. Ravca says, "We greatly prefer a quieter life and the privacy we were deprived of so long. It seems like paradise. We love the air, the mountains, the splendid walks and above all, the people."

Frances Diecks Ravca was elected to NIADA in 1968.

"Easter Sunday." 10 inches. Ready for the Easter Parade.

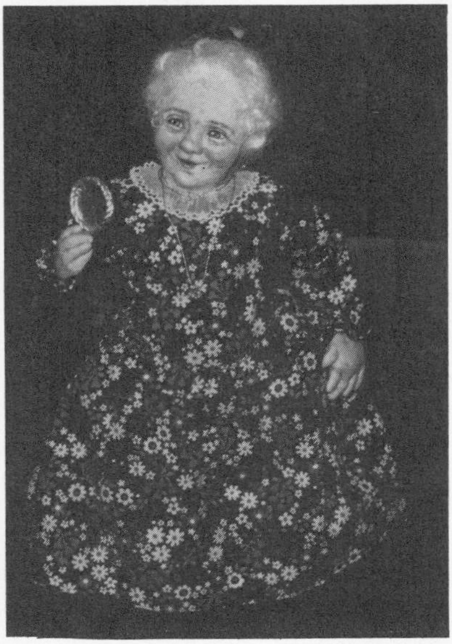

"Primping." 11 inches. One of a series based on same theme.

"Springtime." 12 and 14 inches.

Peddler Woman from Besse, France, by Frances Ravca; Organ-grinder by Bernard Ravca.

"Springtime." Another version.

Bernard and Frances Ravca With Some of Their Dolls.

CHAPTER 23

Fred Thompson

CALIFORNIAN Fred Thompson has sawdust in his beard from a lifetime of working with wood. He has carved, whittled (he hates the word as much as I do for its implication of piddling), sawed, gouged, rasped, and sanded wood nearly as long as he can remember. Many of the reprimands he earned as a boy came from his spending too much time on wood, carving instead of chopping, rather than on his chores.

He and his brothers carved anything; their mother's soap was appropriated as well as the soapstone and chalk from deposits near their home in Cedaredge, Colorado, on the beautiful western slope of the State. All around was an endless supply of soft woods such as cedar, cottonwood roots, and aspen. The boys made all their own toys with their trusty pocketknives.

Fred started serious work in wood by doing "match carving" in the repairing and restoring of antiques; this involved matching grains and ages of wood. As a result he learned a great deal about wood and acquired a deep feeling for it. Exposing a beautiful grain in an exotic wood, he says, gives him a thrilling and unique experience. In addition to his work on furniture, Fred satisfied his urge to work in complete figures by carving large pieces in the free time left after his job as an accountant.

Then tragedy struck. Muscular distrophy put him in the hospital for a long period. He emerged at last, married Sunny Duggan, who had been his nurse, and with her encouragement decided to carve small figures which he could handle. His first nine-inch piece was an Oriental with fancy hairdo and flowing robes. It excited his sister-in-law, an enthusiastic doll collector, who insisted that he could make dolls and sell them. While he dug into all the books on dolls he could find, she wrote to Lewis Sorensen, a charter member of NIADA, about Fred's work. Lewis came to see him and gave him advice and an invitation to a doll show. Ellery Thorpe, another NIADA charter member, also visited and offered suggestions and advice. After Fred sold his first doll, Lewis took several heads to a Chicago exhibition and sold them. Fred was on his way.

He decided to specialize in large people figures measuring from seventeen to twenty-four inches in height, for which he has found a ready market among collectors. His later characters in jellutong wood are his best-known work. He started in 1968 with a twenty-four inch Biblical figure called "The Prophet." The figure was carved of redwood with carved and painted long white hair and beard. The hands were old and gnarled, the feet were clad in carved sandals.

Then he tried a woman, "Marianne Georgian," a large-headed wooden doll in the eighteenth century style. She was also redwood and twenty-four inches tall, but completely different from "The Prophet" with her slim waist, swelling bosom in a lovely carved corset, and carved hair in an elaborate eighteenth century style. Her fully jointed body represented a new challenge to his skill.

Construction was varied to suit the subject. Some torsos were stuffed cloth with heads, lower arms, and lower legs carved of redwood, sugar pine, or maple. Some were all wood, fully jointed, with ball joints at shoulder, elbow, hip, and knee, and had movable heads.

Fred Thompson enjoys making dolls representing artists at their easels with paint tubes and brushes all carved to scale and woodcarvers and other craftsmen at their accustomed benches. All his figures are sanded smooth and many have a hand-rubbed finish. At the end of 1972 he discontinued the use of redwood and has since carved almost exclusively in jellutong wood which is imported from Malasia. It has a close grain with few large markings, and handles more satisfactorily than the coarse-grained but beautiful redwood which is very prone to splintering.

His favorite subjects are very old people of eighty and ninety, "all happy and smiling with miles and miles of character and time in their faces." Each of the larger figures takes more than a hundred hours of work, including the costuming, which Sunny designs and constructs. She became an accomplished seamstress while still in her teens; she also paints in oils. Together they give many programs on their dolls. Fred was elected to NIADA in 1971.

The Shoemaker. Bench and miniature tools are all hand-carved.

Fred Thompson with The Prophet. Doll carved from jellutong wood.

CHAPTER 24

Guy and Virginia Elliott

THE Elliotts were living in Alaska, Guy as sales representative for Wien Air Alaska and Virginia teaching first grade, when dollmaking was thrust upon them. Part of Virginia's work was to arrange displays in the school's main lobby showcase. At Christmas she wanted a large nativity group for the case and enlisted Guy's assistance. They divided the work, Guy making the dolls and Virginia costuming them. The nativity group was a huge success.

The head of one wise man turned out too large so Guy put it aside. Later he decided that the head was just right for an old prospector, so they finished the figure. That was it; they were so excited over the nativity group and the prospector they decided to do more dolls. The next subject was an Eskimo woman performing an ancient dance. So vivid is their portrayal that one can almost hear the rhythm to which the woman bends.

The Eskimo whale hunter which came along soon after stands with harpoon poised and a faraway look in his eyes from scanning endless tundra and sea for game. Then there were the two old Eskimo women sitting side by side on a log; while one sings loudly, the other mocks her.

They did Eskimos, Sourdoughs, Indians, and characters from Robert W. Service's stories. The dolls caught on; not only did summer visitors to Alaska buy them in better gift shops in Fairbanks and Anchorage and in Hickel Hotels throughout the State, but Pan American Airways used Elliott dolls to promote Alaska and the Arctic in their European market. Western Airlines in their West Coast offices also used the dolls to promote Alaskan travel.

Somewhat stunned by all this popularity and the accompanying workload, the Elliotts decided to discontinue their large sales and concentrate on a few quality dolls of artistic merit. They were engaged in such work in 1971 when they left Alaska with their three children and moved to Colorado Springs, Colorado. After finishing up several Alaskan orders, they went on to do Southwest Indians and other characters.

Guy Elliott's art training began with private lessons when he was a boy in San Antonio, Texas. He continued in the Witte Museum's art courses, at California Baptist College, and at the Los Angeles Art Center. He also had on-the-job training along with his commercial art work at Keywest Film Studios and Hecht-Lancaster Productions. He has been a professional artist since 1958 with exhibits in Washington, D.C., San Antonio, Texas, Laguna Beach and Riverside, California.

Virginia Elliott taught sewing classes at home, high school sewing courses, and college courses in advanced sewing. She has made her own clothes since the seventh grade.

Guy was in the Army in Alaska in 1962 when he met Virginia who had been teaching in Fairbanks for five or six years. When his discharge came through in 1963, they were married in a log church during a driving snowstorm dramatized by a colossal Northern Lights display.

Materials for their dolls have been developed over a long period. The nativity group had heads and hands of needle-sculptured nylon stockings mounted on cotton-covered bodies supported by wire armatures and stuffed with cotton. A little later they used beeswax in an experimental move, liked it, and continued its use over the next few years. At present they use poly-clay, a plastic-ceramic combination which molds well and has more durability than the earlier media.

Guy Elliott designs and models the heads and hands and sketches the bodies. Virginia takes over to complete the sewing, stuffing, and supporting of the torso, then follows such sketches and doodles as Guy has turned over to her for the design of the costume. One of the most meaningful compliments Virginia Elliott ever received came from a one hundred nine year old Eskimo woman in Fairbanks. They had made a portrait of the old woman for the Alaska Centennial. She studied the doll a long time and finally said to Virginia, "You sew fur like Eskimo, you make mukluks like Eskimo, you have heart of Eskimo." They were left humble and speechless.

Besides his work on dolls and his commercial art work, until recently Guy has carried out a large volume of free-lance work in commissioned portraits, paintings, and sculpture for a number of Southwest galleries. Virginia has the "small matters" of three children, a household, the correspondence and business side of the operation, and a few other little odds and ends keep her busy, besides making a regular procession of excellent dolls.

In 1973, the Elliotts moved to Lubbock, Texas, where Guy became Minister of Music and Youth in a Baptist Church. Guy and Virginia Elliott were elected to NIADA in 1972.

Virginia and Guy Elliott with Spanish Lady.

The Timberline Trapper. 30 inches.

The Lonesome Traveller. 18 inches.

"Hesitation Before 'Spectoration." Three poised to aim at the Spittoon. Made for the cover of a Western magazine.

CHAPTER 25

Elizabeth Sweet

THE notes on her dollmaking career which I asked Elizabeth Sweet to send me for her monograph were so well written that I merely introduce this artist to you and let her tell her own story. She lives on a mountain in Silverdale, Washington, overlooking the Olympic Mountains and Hood's Canal, with her husband, two Newfoundland dogs, and a large collection of dolls. Here is her story:

Throughout the years I have done some writing, had a few things published, and felt that I was well on my way when I received a letter from Harcourt, Brace and World telling me that they had read one of my short stories and would be interested in seeing a novel.

It was at this crucial moment in my writing career that I happened to complain to my daughter-in-law about the soaring prices of antique dolls, which I collected. "If they get much higher," I said, "I'll have to start making my own." Now this is the sort of remark one might expect to make with impunity, but on Mother's Day I was presented with twenty-five pounds of modeling clay and a set of modeling tools. I was amused, but that was all. No latent talent stirred as I surveyed the gray, sticky stuff. In fact I knew that of all the people in the world I was the one least likely to do anything with a gob of clay.

And I am not, as the expression goes, "just saying that." Prior to this time one of the members of my doll club had told me that in the early days the group used to have contests and that each person was expected to make and bring a doll. When I replied that I was glad this was before my time as a member I meant it with all my heart. Beyond the fact I knew I couldn't possibly make any kind of doll there was a vast disinterest in the whole idea. Nothing, I was sure, could be more boring.

And nothing, I decided, could be more aggravating than trying to find a place to stow away and forget twenty-five pounds of clay in a house already so full that a postcard coming in the mail caused a storage problem.

Watching my effort my husband remarked, "What are you ever going to do with that stuff?"

"Make a doll," I replied with what I thought was great sarcasm.

But apparently he missed the sarcasm and when he kindly tried to explain to me that I would be wasting my time I was outraged! Of course, I knew I couldn't make a doll but for him to say so was treachery!

My first effort turned out to be "Old Woman at Church," a passable doll but still in clay form. From that first step many people helped me along. From an artist and a wonderful person, Lillian Smart, I was able to borrow books on the composition of wax, and thus come up with my own formula which is tough, durable, and impervious even to freezing and to all but direct heat.

From Ada Odenrider, another artist and a grand person, I learned to make molds.

After wax I dabbled in papier mache. A friend gave me an old Milliner's Model body, so of course I made a head for it. Another friend commissioned me to make an entire doll for her. I believe that had it not been for this encouragement my new career might have died stillborn, because while I enjoy creating dolls (or I wouldn't do it) the fact that someone was willing to pay good money for them was proof that it was not only in my own imagination that my "children" were succeeding. I abandoned papier mache because I was never able to get the smooth effect I wanted.

I then modeled a little girl, Jennifer, and wanted to try her in bisque. Back I went to Ada who, busy as she is, is never too busy to help a friend. From nine in the morning until eleven that night we went through a crash course in pouring, cleaning, firing, painting, and glazing. In between we found time to rush out and buy my kiln and the other supplies I would need for Jennifer.

I went on with Amy and Julie, each in a series of ten dolls; each doll having her name and number incised in the bisque. Others followed, mostly in limited editions.

My acceptance into NIADA in 1968 was such a big moment that I considered having "NIADA" tattooed on my forehead, but managed to restrain myself.

Elizabeth Sweet failed to mention she is two or three years behind on orders, but not as far behind as she is on the novel Harcourt, Brace and World suggested she write ten or twelve years ago. Pages of this novel are still on her desk, mixed up with letters from doll collectors, doll pictures, and NIADA letters. She has been dogged by illness for several years but is now back at work on her distinctive dolls.

Julie.

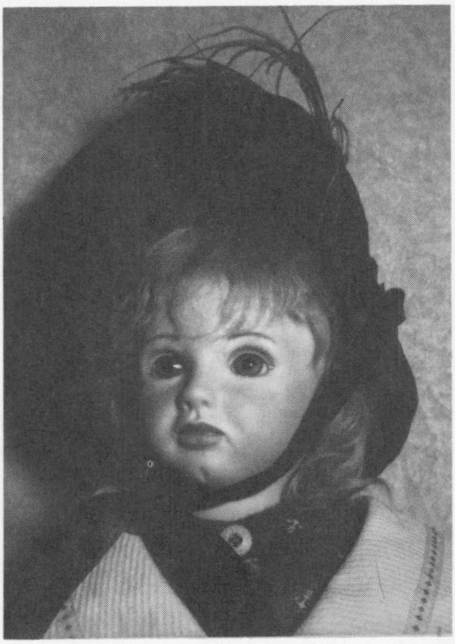

Amy.

Nora. Older sister of Julie.

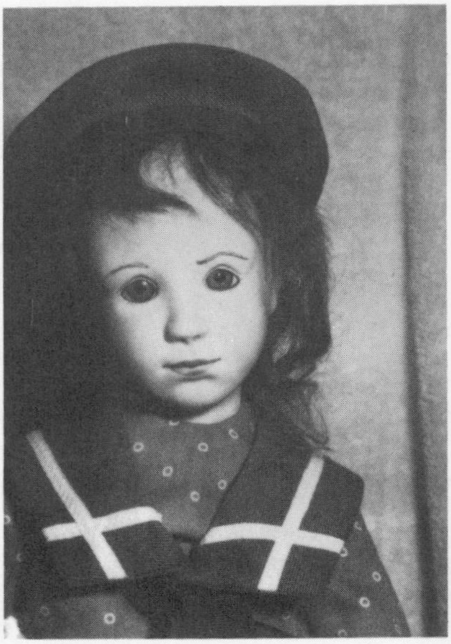

Charles Edward.

Jennifer.

Laura.

Beth Ann.

Elizabeth Sweet with Original Wax Baby Albert.

CHAPTER 26

Marianne de Nunez

THE gorgeous young playground instructor with his slim golden tan figure, blue eyes, and blond hair introduced the little group of children to horned toads and papier mache. Marianne de Nunez loved the toad but the sticky, messy papier mache was purely marvelous; soon she was in it up to her elbows. Wanting approval from the handsome instructor, she busily built up the stuff on a dowel, let it harden a bit as he had instructed, then carefully modeled a doll. She was in the third grade and she never forgot her first doll.

A year later her family returned from California to Toledo, Ohio, where she had been born. There she attended class at the Toledo Museum of Art in an endowed art school which accepted gifted students from grade schools for Saturday classes. She was eight when she painted a tempera painting of an Egyptian woman which caused the teachers to admit her to the adult classes. Besides giving a wider choice of subjects, the adult classes met after school as well as on Saturdays. Because of a carving she had made she was put in the puppetry class and loved every minute of it. Her Donald Duck was carved of wood with articulated limbs and a moving, quacking bill, and was dressed in a proper sailor suit. Then came a one-eyed pirate molded in plastic wood.

She also studied tempera and oil painting, figure drawing, ceramics, and other subjects, and modeled for fashion classes. She literally grew up in an art museum, attending two or three classes a week, and also majored in art in high school. She graduated from high school at sixteen and then married Roger Griswold.

One of her early jobs was as an industrial designer in which she also made scale models of some of the designs. She had bluffed her way into the job, not knowing what a plan view was, but soon learning to render in perspective to scale. If the office in Toledo had not been closed, she would have remained at the job. After that she did some fashion modeling.

Marianne, her husband, and small son moved a great deal, once from Toledo to Florida and back in less than a year. At one time she had completely redecorated an old building for an antique shop to the point of being ready to open when off they moved to another place and another job for her husband. Finally, in Toledo her husband started selling vacuum cleaners and opened his own shop where Marianne learned to repair the machines. This lasted only a year and she hated it. On they went to California, where Marianne worked at decorating expensive dishes for several years, making good money at piece rates, but driving herself so hard that she had to quit because of an ulcer, colitis, and a severe case of arthritis of the back and wrist. The arthritis is still with her. She supervised thirty children in a riding club during that time and then became a draftsman at Lockheed. After a year of this she divorced her husband and married Val de Nunez.

On a trip to Mexico, they saw some plasticine caricatures which so intrigued Val that he had one done of himself. Val had a small shop on Olvera Street in downtown Los Angeles. A large restaurant wanted caricatures of their employees and Val talked them into three-dimensional caricatures. He is better on paper, so Marianne finally took over and made them. She used colored plasticine and working from photographs proved so time consuming (and at a mere ten dollars apiece!) that she gave up. The finished figures were put on display and were seen by someone making a movie tentatively titled "Witchcraft." He wanted a set of Voodoo dolls with the faces of Robert Alda, Neil Hamilton, and Linda Christian. They were about eighteen inches tall, and one had a soft plug in the forehead to admit a hatpin, as it was supposed to be stabbed. There were six dolls in all and she had ten days in which to make them. The film was released three years later under another title but was so bad few remember it.

In searching for wigs for these dolls she had found a doll hospital which could also furnish a body for an old Armand

Marseille doll she had long cherished and which she had despaired of restoring. The shop owner gave her a doll very much like a Lenci with velvet limbs and she restored it so well that it looked like new. Her friends admired it and urged her to set up professional doll repair service. In her search for old doll parts for restoration work she found an ad offering antique doll parts in quantity and bought the lot. While carrying on restoration jobs, she bought a kiln and experimented with bisque dolls, making her first bisque head in 1959. By 1962, she had two original dolls in porcelain, which she exhibited at the UFDC Convention in Buffalo that year.

Since then Marianne de Nunez has created two more originals, both as elegantly executed as the first two. Three have the fine kid bodies which she makes with professional precision. The faces are marvelously alive and glowing, and the characterizations are strong and convincing. Poor health has dogged her for the past few years and greatly interferes with her work. In 1971, Marianne de Nunez was elected to NIADA.

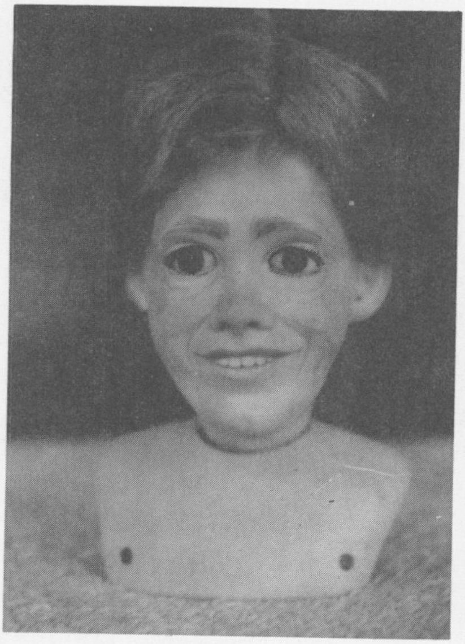

Pedlar Head. (Shown on incorrect shoulder plate)

Pedlar Woman.

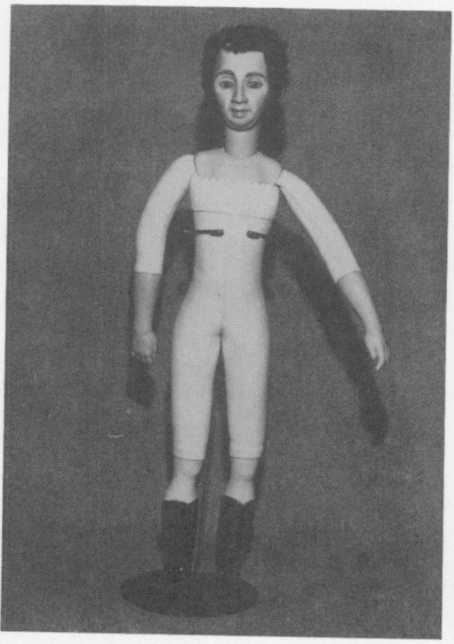

Cyril. All-kid body.

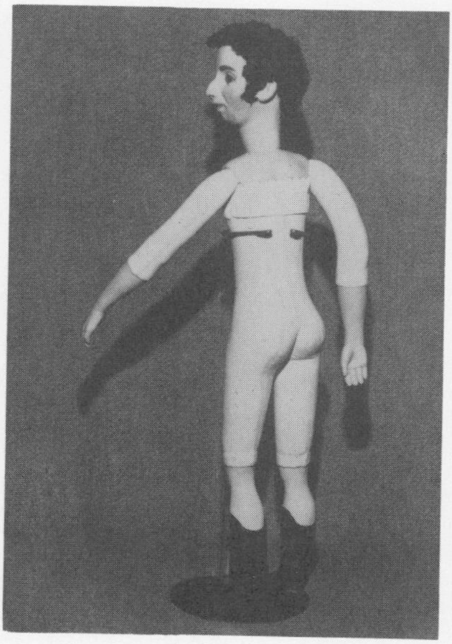

Cyril.

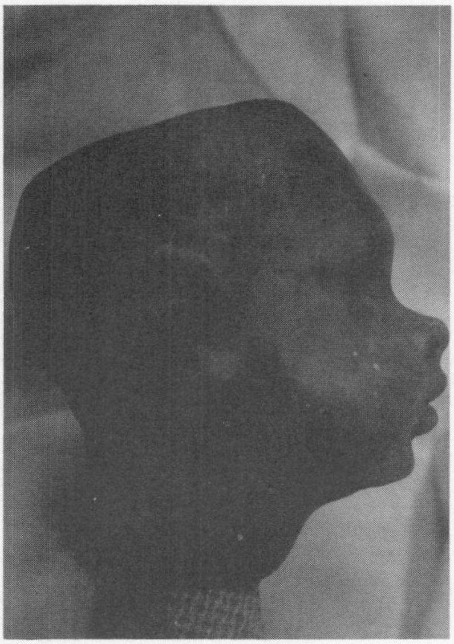

Jasmine Profile.

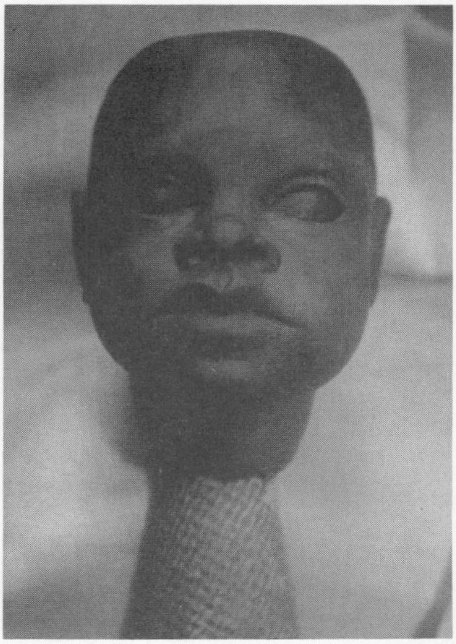

Original modeled gray pottery clay head for Jasmine.

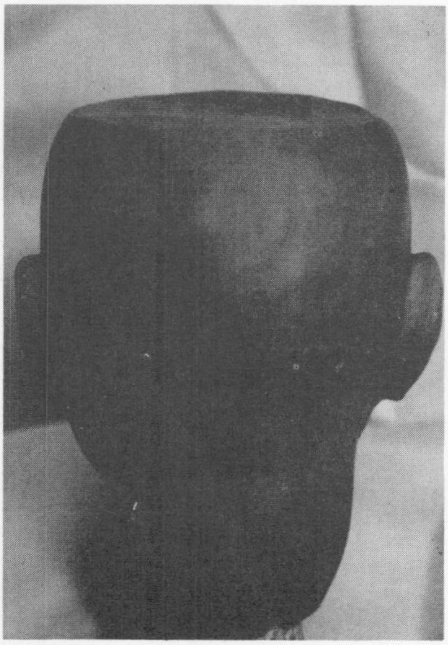

Back of Jasmine Head with Incised "Marianne."

Jasmine. Head, arms, and legs cast in porcelain; stuffed cloth torso.

CHAPTER 27

Diana Lence Crosby

DIANA LENCE became interested in art early in life. Her posters received prizes, but her great interest was in modeling horses. She began attending doll conventions with her mother, Fidelia Lence, UFDC President, 1971-73, when she was seventeen and her interest in dolls grew with each convention. Her first doll, "Miss Unity," the Federation emblem, was costumed in blue like the original and mounted on a black stand. Copies were sold for the benefit of the UFDC quarterly magazine, *Doll News.*

After graduating in animal husbandry from the University of Massachusetts, she studied art at the Boston Museum of Fine Arts while working in the field of cancer research with animals. In 1959 she married a classmate, Donald F. Crosby, and they soon moved to Ohio to raise beef cattle. While there Diana worked with a fine teacher on porcelain molding and china painting. After her son Dana was born, she returned to dollmaking.

Soon after they were back in Boston and the Boston UFDC convention committee needed a souvenir doll head for the 1967 national convention. Diana Crosby submitted the Priscilla Alden head on which she was then working and was commissioned to make one thousand of them in porcelain to be used as souvenirs of the convention. When the Detroit convention came along in 1970, she made eight hundred heads of an antique type for the souvenir, called "Mlle. Detroit." When she recovered from this second large order, she finished John Alden and two children to go with Priscilla. Among her other dolls are Abraham Lincoln, Clara Barton, Scarlett O'Hara, several French ladies after fashion prints of 1810 to 1860, and a new series of "The Belles of Fashion."

Diana Lence Crosby was voted a member of NIADA in 1968 and now lives with her husband and three children in Griffin, Georgia.

City Boy and Country Boy.

The Pilgrim Family.

Diana Lence Crosby with a "Belle of Fashion."

CHAPTER 28

Rene Harrison

RENE HARRISON of Louisiana spent many years reproducing the antique dolls she loved before she started designing her own dolls. Specializing in portrait dolls, she chooses well-known figures whose personalities interest her. Her porcelain medium is ideally suited to the delicate effects in which she delights.

Rene and her husband E. G., have moved about the country because of his work. When their two sons grew up she abandoned the photography for which she had been trained in favor of dolls and has been completely absorbed in dollmaking ever since. Her early portrait of her mother, Ethel Shockley, at age twenty-one received the approval of her older brothers and sisters and Rene was encouraged to go on to other portraits.

Rene Harrison's dolls are made of the finest porcelain and painted with imported Dresden china paints. They are put through three or four firings in order to achieve a fine smooth finish. Heads and lower arms are porcelain, and bodies cotton stuffed muslin. What began as a hobby has become a profitable occupation. She now specializes in portraits of personages, most of them American and ranging widely over the American scene. She expresses a preference for nineteenth century dolls and is likely to work on those her mood dictates. Her dolls are sold both dressed and undressed.

She says, "All the frustrations of life recede and time is like a vapor when I have a piece of clay in my hands."

Rene Harrison was elected to NIADA in 1969.

Chucky.

Period Ladies; Left, 1850; right, 1900.

Felice.

Rene Harrison Holding 1837 Lady; 1830 Lady Standing.

CHAPTER 29

Frank and Elizabeth Haines

FRANK AND ELIZABETH HAINES have always worked as a team. Their special subject is a unique series of brides illustrating bridal customs from 1600 B.C. A serious study of marriage and the status of women throughout the ages provided the background for their work. Frank Haines, a gifted sculptor, shapes the eighteen-inch figures from a durable composition. Each figure is an individual character study of the beauty type of the period or the portrait of a historical personage. Elizabeth Haines does the research, designs and makes the costumes, paints the faces, and makes the wigs.

There are only four white veils among the twenty-four brides of their four groups! One group includes Bibiyah of Babylonia, 1600 B.C.; the Druid bride, Gyptis of Gaul, 600 B.C.; Melina of Athens, 451 B.C.; Catarina of Venice, 959 A.D.; Elise of France, 1350 A.D.; and Giovanna Cenami of Flanders, 1434 A.D. Another group consists of Nefertiti of Egypt, 1375 B.C., showing marriage by civil contract; Octavia of the Early Roman Empire, 500 B.C., showing pagan religious marriage; Geertruda, a Chieftain's bride, Teutons, 500 A.D., marriage by purchase; Demoiselle Angelique of France, 1250 A.D., marriage at church door; Lady Mary Margaret (seven years old) of England, 1565 A.D., child marriage; and Marie-Louise of France, 1720 A.D., custom of escorting bride to bed.

The first American group has Anne Burras of Jamestown, 1608, first English bride in North America; Susanna White-Winslow of Plymouth, first Pilgrim bride, 1620; Lyzbet van Loos of New

Amsterdam, 1640-50, Dutch patroon bride; Mary MacTavish of Pennsylvania, 1650-75, Scots-Irish frontier bride; Cecily Rose of New Jersey, 1812, "Coming Out Bride"; and Rebecca Reeves, Philadelphia, 1820, a Quaker bride.

The second American series has Catalina de Valdes of St. Augustine, 1594, first recorded bride in the colony; Pocahontas of Jamestown, 1614, most famous native American bride; Lady Anne of Maryland, 1640, Cavalier bride; Hannah Hull of Boston, 1676, unusual dowry; Lady Henrietta of New York, 1690, records England's acquisition of New Amsterdam; and Lisette Clanet of New Orleans, 1728, honors "casette" girls. Armegot Printz of New Sweden, 1665, first Christian bride in present Pennsylvania, heads the third American series.

The original research for this unique work on brides and bridal customs required a year of research in history, law, religion, folklore, and costume. Then each bride was selected and researched extensively before work could begin on the doll itself. Created especially for programs for women's groups, the four series of dolls were used to illustrate lectures given by Betty Haines throughout Pennsylvania and the Eastern states while living in Philadelphia; and more recently in the Wilmington, North Carolina, area.

Lest anyone think that all this education and history are excellent but dull, I quote some choice bits from the story of the Druid bride, Gyptis:

> The Druid philosophy of life and death caused them to mourn at weddings and rejoice at funerals, for troubles begun and troubles ended. And their brides dressed accordingly—yes, in black.
>
> The bride was bought from her parents and after the wedding ceremony the priest walked beside her, chanting, "From this day forth, young wife, thou alone will have to bear the burden of your united household. You will have to attend the baking oven; provide fule and go in search of food; you will have to prepare the resinous torch and the lamp. You will attend the cow and even the horse if your husband requires it."
>
> What the husband did, it doesn't say, and for her things steadily got no better: "Always full of respect, you will wait upon him, standing behind him at his meals. If he chooses to take more wives, you will receive your new companions with sweetness. If he is angry with you and strikes you, you will pray to Esus, the only God, but you will never blame your husband, who cannot do wrong. If he wishes to take you to war, you will carry his baggage, keep his arms in good condition, and nurse him if he should be sick or wounded. Happiness consists in the fulfillment of duty. Be happy, my child!"

Small wonder that this one-of-a-kind, museum-quality collection is shown frequently to women's organizations, rented for displays in stores (where it is often the feature of bridal shows) and banks, or placed as a loan exhibit in art galleries. Newspaper and magazine coverage has been constant and wide. Recently the brides were featured in the *Christian Science Monitor* and the Associated Press' Special Bride Supplement.

Figures have been completed for a third series of "Marriage Forms," as the antique groups are titled. Increasing interest in their brides has caused the Haineses to make available limited editions of some of the dolls in their American series.

The Haineses, both Philadelphians, studied art at the Philadelphia School of Industrial Art (now the Philadelphia Museum School of Art). Frank specialized in water color and for fifteen years made annual trips abroad to study sculpture, painting, and antique furniture in museums and galleries in Europe. Character studies are his *metier.*

Elizabeth specialized in historic costume and design, and has researched in museums and libraries both here and abroad. She studied dramatics with private teachers and members of the Orpheum and Chicago theatrical stock companies, as well as researching theatre history and puppet history. She learned to sew from a professional modiste.

The couple's first career was in marionettes, which they made and operated for thirty-four years in their own theatre and on tour around the Eastern seaboard. They made their own marionettes; each was an individual, a hand-carved character study, dressed in authentic costume. Combined with his ability as a sculptor, Frank Haines has a strong mechanical bent which enabled him to create marionettes with unusually smooth and fluid action. Betty Haines costumed the puppets and created specially adapted plays and skits.

Working in the tradition of the European marionette theatre, where puppetry is an art, they created animated carved marionettes with charm and beauty, rather than the caricature or comic types more familiar in America. Besides their use in performance, the Haines Marionettes have been used by local national advertisers, and have appeared on live television and in commercial movies. The Canadian Government, the New York State Department of

Agriculture, and the Pennsylvania State Medical Association have employed them in teaching and promotion.

From 1933 to 1967 the Haineses made all the hand-puppets, sets, and props used by an organization of milk dealers, the Dairy Council, Inc., for a milk promotion and health education program in the elementary schools of Pennsylvania, New Jersey, Delaware, and Maryland. The puppet shows, given by the Dairy Council's Dramatic Department, were an important feature of their work. During these years the Haineses made nearly seven hundred hand puppets, and numerous props such as tractors, Alaskan dog sleds, Irish wicker donkey carts, grand pianos, circus wagons, and dental office equipment.

In 1947 Encyclopedia Britannica engaged them to make a teaching film, "Making Marionettes," selecting them over competing New York and Chicago groups. Betty Haines writes:

> Of all our happy and sometimes hectic experiences, the two which we treasure most are our annual Christmas show at the Overbrook School for the Blind in Philadelphia and our work with mentally ill veterans at the Valley Forge Veterans Hospital, both a first in our field. A friend interested us in giving shows for the blind, as there was little "live" entertainment for them at that time. We began by having them come to our studio dress rehearsals, and we created special techniques in playing for them. We chose acts with dialogue which carried the action, sometimes rewriting the scripts to include indirect description, as when the Gingerbread Boy called to the wolf, "Here I am, *up on the wall.*" By removing the padding from the stage floor, we made it possible for the children to hear the puppets moving about. We wanted them to feel they were experiencing the same thing sighted children did. From what the school's director and teachers told us and the reactions of the children, it seems we succeeded. Attendance at the studio shows, which was used as a reward for good behavior, increased so much that the administration asked us to take our shows to the school so the entire student body could "see" them. They were wonderful audiences for they knew how to listen and were aware of the slightest inflection and nuance.
>
> One summer the Red Cross asked us to start a hand-puppet project for critically disturbed patients at Valley Forge Veterans' Hospital. We welcomed the opportunity. From the beginning we never urged the men to enter into the program. We did an introductory show by doing some marionette dancing numbers on top of a table and showing some hand-puppets made for the Dairy Council. We told them we were there to work with them on making some hand-puppets if they'd like to. The fact that we came to them voluntarily "from the outside" helped.
>
> We worked in the locked wards with the most disturbed patients, and it was a tremendous challenge. One had to be absolutely honest, for they detected and suspected any subterfuge or unearned praise. We

treated them as though they were normal. When a patient said, "Boy, is that ever a lousy ear," we agreed that it was, but added, "You've done very well with the nose," or whatever feature they had done well.

Of course, the hand-puppets were very simple. We devised an egg-shaped head from plastic wood, which we supplied, as the men had to have a base on which to start. Then they built up the features with more plastic wood, which we supplied, and painted the faces with show-card colors. The plain little "costumes" were made at home by Red Cross volunteers on our patterns, and we used old hospital sheets to make small backdrops also painted with showcard colors. Some patients made puppets; some painted backdrops; some helped plan THE SHOW; and eventually nearly all got into the act. This is the great value of puppets in work of this sort; there is bound to be something that will appeal to everyone.

We even put on a show, borrowing a stage from the Dairy Council. The doctors were delighted when one of the most withdrawn patients chose to be part of it. (He didn't mind because he was hidden by the backdrop.) According to Army records, this was the first time such a project had been tried and carried out successfully in a Service hospital and we're grateful we could be a part of it.

The couple also were responsible for the first modern performance in this country of "Music and Marionettes" in the style of the eighteenth century marionette theatre in which singers and musicians perform backstage and puppets synchronize with them, the audience seeing only the puppets (Premiere, Cosmopolitan Club, Philadelphia, 1936); the first advertising at a medical convention to show the advantages to both family and mentally retarded child of placing the child in a special school; and the first "radio marionettes" and marionette shows for a radio studio audience, performed simultaneously while broadcasting (WOKO, Philadelphia, 1939-40).

Their marionette collection of one hundred seventy-five hand-carved figures, complete with staging, sets, and scripts is going to the Smithsonian Institution, to be housed at the recently acquired Cooper-Hewitt Museum, New York, now called the National Museum of Design. They are the first American marionettes to be permanently represented there.

When they ended their marionette activities and turned to people figures, Frank and Elizabeth Haines put to use all they had learned in this medium in the creation of new subjects. A spectacular one-of-a-kind project was the creation of life-sized carved wooden figures of the Holy Family dressed in fabric costumes in the manner of the Renaissance creche. Made for the Blaffer Trust in New Harmony, Indiana, they were loaned to the National Shrine of Our Lady of the Snows in Belleville, Illinois, during 1959-61 and drew over twenty-six thousand visitors during the Christmas season.

Frank and Elizabeth Haines now work full time making new dolls for their "Wedding Belles" series and exhibiting the four completed groups. They were voted into NIADA in 1971.

Geertruda. Tuetonic Chieftain's Bride, 500 A.D.

Pocahontas. Jamestown, 1614.

Cecily Rose. New Jersey, 1812.

Lisette Clanet. New Orleans, 1728.

Frank and Elizabeth Haines with Group "B" Brides. L to R: Bibyah, Babylon; Elise, France; Melina, Greece; Gyptis, Gaul; Catarina, Venice; Giovanna, Flanders.

Handpuppets used in sketch, "Whale Ho!" (Note wrist of operator behind the captain).

Hansel, Gretel, and the Witch Marionettes.

CHAPTER 30

Jacques and France Rommel

WHEN a dedicated aesthete who is a professor of art meets a Parisian reared close to the world of fashion, one may expect fireworks something like the original Rommel dolls. Not for these two the careful, safe, solid heads with bisymmetrical painted features; they prefer an evocative, mysteriously beautiful face barely indicated on the fabric-sculptured head and veiled with delicate silk mousseline so that a mere suggestion of features is achieved. Without realistic detail the nearly featureless face crowns a body so skillfully positioned its particular message is clear to the most casual glance.

The rich and intricate costuming is carried out by France Rommel who, like all little girls of Paris, had learned fine sewing at an early age. Then, too, her mother had been curator of a Loire Valley castle and was a sophisticated doll collector. France grew up knowing fine dolls intimately.

Together the Rommels plan and construct each doll, combining Jacques' sound aesthetic feelings and training with France's skill. Fabric over a wire armature is the basic material. To achieve the desired elegance the same involvement, skill, and search for beauty demanded of any work of art is required. In each creation the subject itself determines the exact "palette" of fabrics, laces, furs, and feathers which will be used.

"The first doll was 'born' in 1968," writes Jacques. "Inspired by a friend who was proficient in creating papier mache angels, France had been tempted into creating some in her own style.

Soon, reacting to the inertness of the papier mache, she shifted to actually dressing the figures with fabrics. The first creation represented a shepherd, a frankly awkward creature, but the first shy step into doll creation. Continually supported but also relentlessly analyzed and criticized, she began to improve in craftsmanship and aesthetics. France and I argued for a long time about the importance of features; our overall purpose, we decided, was the creation of haute-couture in miniature, not toys but objets d'art.

"With all the aesthetic implications of this goal in mind, each creation has to answer for itself with its own quality, just as any model of haute-couture has to convey its own beauty. In fact, the lightly suggested features are there only to open a window to the viewer, so that he may participate and imagine the features he desires; for the absence of precisely defined features is an invitation to dream. The objective of quality is reached when a lovely-lively little person is brought into existence."

Jacques Rommel's credits include an impressive list of one-man shows in Europe, North and Central Africa, and the United States. He has shown in a long list of world festivals and performed on radio and television programs from Yugoslavia to France to the United States. Besides his work as Professor of Art, M. Rommel has for many years maintained his own Atelier Rommel in Africa, in France, and in Farmington, Connecticut. His paintings are in collections on five continents, and the prestigious Academie Francaise awarded the Prix Archon 1960 to his book *Poesie.*

France and Jacques Rommel became NIADA Associate Members in 1974.

Three Dressed-up Lovelies: 1900, 1850, 1834.

Mae West. 1933.

Mistinguette. 1913.

Francoise. 1898.

Suzanne. ca. 1879.

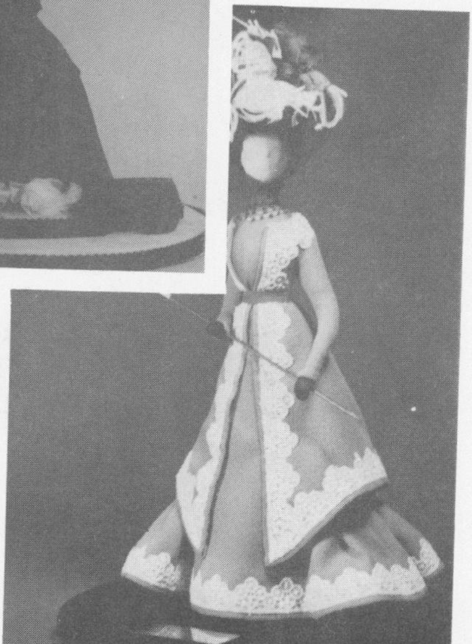

Races Dress. 1899.

Jacques and France Rommel With Sophie in Gala Costume of 1881.

CHAPTER 31

Laura Alleman

THE elderly people figures of Laura Alleman of Utah won blue ribbons at three UFDC conventions and were displayed widely before she applied to NIADA. Her love of activity is expressed in her dolls, which are conceived in pairs or trios doing something gently amusing. There is, for example, an old man trying to sew a button on his "longies" while being almost crowded out of the scene by the clutter of dolls his wife is making. Alleman's medium is fine kidskin stretched over a head molded of plastic wood. The body is a wire armature covered with sculptured cotton and finished in kid. Sizes range from sixteen inches to twenty-two inches.

Laura Alleman arrived at this point after many forays into other doll media. There were the very early hollyhock ladies floating down the pasture stream in their green cucumber boats, the soap people who wound up in the Saturday night tub, the cornshuck dolls with cornsilk hair which frizzled uncontrollably when dry, and the braided straw people who stubbornly refused to assume natural positions. For a while she gave up experimenting.

After graduating from Brigham Young University, she married, and brought up three children. The sudden death of her grown daughter and her only son within thirteen months left her sorely in need of something to fill the void so she turned to dolls. For a while she helped a dollmaker with body work; then, having read about apple dolls in a newspaper, she confiscated some fruit destined for her husband's lunch and carved her first apple heads.

After making and selling several, she began experimenting in other media. Doll collecting friends, *The American Doll Artist,* a doll club, and a trip to a UFDC convention completed her turnabout to more serious dolls, first wood and then her present medium.

Laura Alleman was elected to NIADA in 1974.

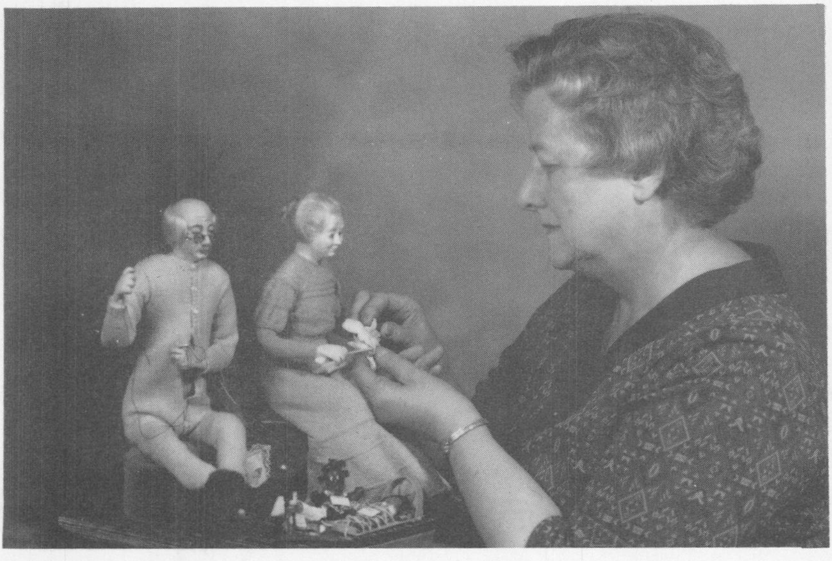

Laura Alleman Adds Finishing Touches to "Christmas Priorities." 16 inches. Grandpa attempts own mending while Grandma is occupied with making Christmas dolls.

"Dolly's New Cradle." 4, 11, 16 inches. Grandpa presents Granddaughter with new doll cradle he has made.

"In Sickness and In Health." 18 inches. Grandma administers home remedies to Grandpa who is soaking his feet in a mustard bath.

CHAPTER 32

Carol Nordell

CAROL NORDELL'S doll subjects are wide-ranging and include people figures from famous portraits, primitive paintings, the ballet, and opera. Her material requires a wrapped wire armature with a small styrofoam ball placed on the neck as a base for the head, which is modeled over it in a special, durable composition. Using the same substance, the hands are modeled on the end of the wired and wrapped arm. The feet are formed around magnets so they will stand on metal without vertical support. Miniatures fascinate Carol and she has made many in various scales.

Carol took art courses in college and has since taken many more. She married Jack Nordell several months before he was shipped overseas in World War II. Care of her three children and home at Mount Vernon, New York, have filled many years. There have also been five litters of Siberian husky pups, four of which still dominate her household. While her girls were in college she had a thriving home baking and food-decorating business, during which she made her first dolls of gingerbread. They were frosted and elaborately decorated and proved so popular she had to give decorating classes after she closed the business. She began painting seriously, but gave up when she found sales slow. Drawn by the challenge and basic seriousness of interpreting various kinds of people in doll form, she has succumbed to their charm and finds ideas for new figures coming faster than she can possibly work them out. Carol Nordell was elected to NIADA in 1974.

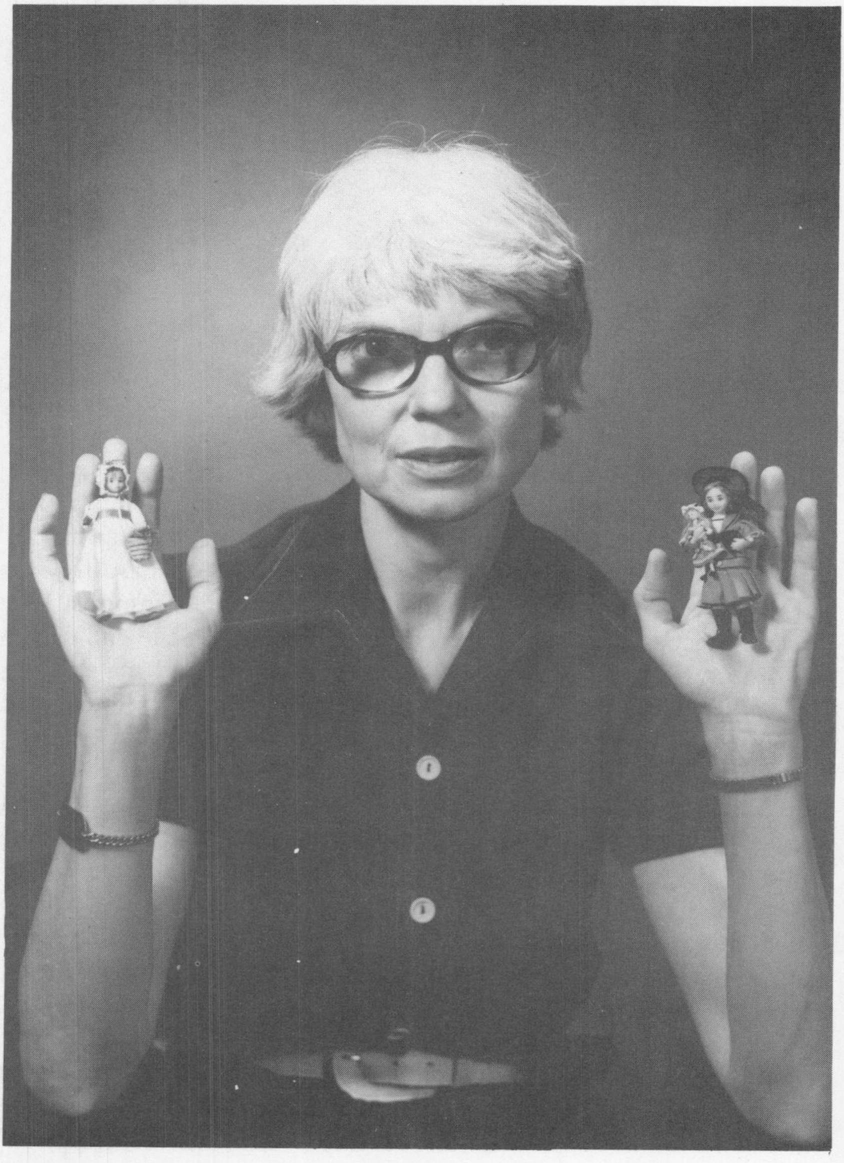

Carol Nordell With Two Little Girls. 3½ inches.

Little Buttercup. 10 inches, wax. From "Pinafore."

Elizabeth Copley. 7 inches. From the Copley painting.

Mrs. Freake and Baby Mary. Woman, 10 inches, wax. From the unsigned American oil painting of 1674.

APPENDIX

Catalog of the Artists' Dolls

THE figures shown in parentheses represent the total number of dolls produced in each model at this writing. In some cases it was impossible to establish the exact number of dolls produced. In these instances no quantity is given or an approximation is given.

CATALOG OF VANEK DOLLS

Porcelain, fully jointed, or porcelain head and limbs on muslin body. Each doll is copyrighted, numbered, dated, and signed.

1971 *Baby Peter.* 7" sitting. All porcelain, ball-jointed at hip and shoulder, molded hair, painted eyes, dressed in romper suit.

Little Leaguer. 14". All porcelain, ball-jointed, molded hair, painted eyes. Baseball suit, wooden bat.

Modern Troubador. 14". All porcelain, ball-jointed, painted eyes, blond Dynel wig, molded boots. Dressed in bell-bottom pants, leather vest, flaired shirt, beads, with guitar.

Diamond Lil. 16". Porcelain head and limbs on muslin fashion body. Pierced ears, glass eyes, real lashes, platinum Dynel wig. Shimmering lined dress, hat, feather boa, and jewelry.

1972 *Charlie Chaplin.* 16". All porcelain, ball-jointed at shoulder, elbow, hip, and head. Bowler hat, characteristic costume, and boots.

1973 *Tom Sawyer.* 16" sitting. All porcelain, fully articulated at shoulders, elbows, hips, knees, and neck, so that he can do many things. Freckled face, human hair, straw hat, fishpole, trout.

Dewees Cochran. 14" sitting. Porcelain head and limbs on muslin body, painted eyes, Saran wig. Shown working on one of her "Look-Alikes." Chair by Carl Hansen. Limit–12.

Catalog of Cerepak Dolls

Various materials, individually noted.

1964 *Kindergarten Book Characters.* (41) Like Dick, Jane, and Sally. Fabric, wired with pipe cleaners, felt or painted eyes, yarn wigs.

Fairy Tale Characters. Construction similar to first dolls but stronger wires in body and oil paints used on faces.

1965 *Dolls of Many Nations.* (39) Mostly felt, stuffed with cotton and rise (to facilitate posing), yarn wigs.

Story Characters. (27) Like Robin Hood, Peter Pan, and Captain Hook. Body frame wrapped mummy-style; experimented with papier mache and liquid rubber.

1966 *United States Presidents.* 14-20". (35) Some papier mache covered with liquid rubber, some self-drying clays and balsa wood carvings. Many taped wire bodies, painted with enamels, Dynel wigs.

1967 *Nursery Rhyme Characters.* (47) With full background scenery. Fabric with felt stuffed bodies, wired to pose.

Hubert Humphrey. *Nelson Rockefeller.*
George Romney. *Mark Twain.*
Ben Franklin. *Jacqueline Kennedy.*

And others. Balsa and pear woods.

1969 *President Nixon.* To add to 1966 group.

United States Presidents. 30-36". Various woods and wood putty with bodies jointed at elbows, wrists, and knees with movable heads, redwood legs, and cast plaster hands on bodies of stuffed felt over wire armatures. Wigs layered in grooves on heads.

Manikins. Window displays. Foam balls covered with water putty. Variety of characters including pixies, sea divers, Eskimos, and scarecrows.

1970 *Sugar-Sugar and Honey-Honey.* 16" and 18". Wood putty, glass eyes, dacron-stuffed bodies, acrylic plush hair.

Sugar-Plum. 30". Water putty over foam ball. Children's clothes manikin.

Goldy Locks and Three Bears. 12" girl. Balsa wood and wood putty, jointed, stuffed bodies.

1971 *Pixie.* 9½". All ceramic with incised wings and pants. Limit–12.

Kim. 14". All ceramic, open mouth, singing. Limit–15.

1972 *Jahn.* 13½". Little goose boy, jointed ceramic. Limit–6.

Lynn. 14". Sister to Kim. Jointed ceramic. Limit–6.

Peaches and Patty Cake. 7½". Small baby dolls, all ceramic. Molded hair. Limit–12 each.

Puddin' and Patches. 9". Novelty elfin children. Ceramic. Limit–10 each.

Nancy. 14". Pouty portrait doll. All bisque, jointed, glass eyes. Limit–6.

1974 *Norman.* 14". Toddler baby boy. All bisque, jointed, glass eyes. Limit–6.

CATALOG OF BRINGLOE DOLLS

Hand-carved heads and hands, body parts for jointed figure first turned on lathe, later on automatic lathe, all of Alaskan cedar; unless otherwise noted. Duplicates of each design not noted; total of approximately one thousand six hundred figures made to date.

1947-50 *Cloth Dolls.* Made as gifts. Molded faces, cloth-covered.

1950-52 *Pioneer Family in Everyday Dress.* Father, mother, boy, girl. Wooden faces and hands, cloth bodies with wire armature. Original group for Washington State Museum.

Christmas Tree Angels. Same construction. For gifts.

Puget Sound Indian Family. Father, mother, and baby in cradle. First jointed wood bodies.

Pioneer Family in Sunday Dress. Father, mother, boy, girl. Original for Seattle Public Schools.

Pioneer Couples in Sunday Dress.

1953 *Princess Angeline and Chief Seattle.* (3 pairs) Early Seattle figures.

Baby Jesus. (1) Scale 2" to 1'. Jointed wood.

1955 *Lewis and Clark Expedition Group.* (9 sets) Seven figures. Original group for Washington State Park Commission in Fort Columbia Museum. Eight duplicate groups for St. Louis Public Schools.

Robert and Crew. Ten figures depicting discovery of the mouth of the Columbia River. Original at Fort Columbia Museum, Washington State Parks Commission.

Pilgrim Family in Everyday Dress. Father, mother, boy, girl.

Pilgrim Family in Sunday Dress. Same as above.

Northwest Coast Indian Costumes. Designed and made costumes for Encyclopedia Britannica film, "Indians of Long Ago." Northwest section.

1957 *Prehistoric Indians.* Of the Columbia Basin. For diorama installation, Ginko State Park, Washington State Parks Commission.

Northwest Coast Indians in Ceremonial Dress. San Francisco Schools.

1960 *Indians and Fur Trappers.* Ten figures for diorama at Fort Okanagon State Park, Washington State Parks Commission.

Shoshone Indians, Fur Trappers, Smoke Jumper. Diorama for the Mobile Museum unit of the United States Forest Service, Ogden, Utah, Sector.

1966 *Assyrian King and Parasol Bearer.*
Mayan Priest and Attendant.
Egyptian Magistrate and Scribe.
Early Man, Prehistoric. (5)
Khmer King, Queen, Woman, Servant.
Astronauts.
Two Cretan Women.
Roman Matron and Man.
Egyptian Peasant.
Prehistoric Arizona Indians.
Stonehenge Man.

The above 1966 figures were made for the Illinois State University Museum for diorama installation.

1969 *Military Figures.* (5) Showing uniforms of the United States Army for the Milwaukee Public Museum.

Gabriel. *Evangeline.*
La Salle. *Pere Marquette.*
Casquette Girl. *Bienville.*
Louisiana figures for New Orleans Public Schools.

1970 *Anthony Wayne.* *Father Gabriel Richard.*
Chief Pontiac. *Dr. Martin Luther King, Jr.*
George Washington Carver. *Ralph Bunche.*
Antoine de la Mothe Cadillac and Madame Cadillac.
Teaching aids for the Detroit Children's Museum.
Standing Earth. Menomini Chief.

1972 *Buffalo Bill.*
Klondike Goldrush Figures. Erastus Brainard, George Carmack, "Soapy" Smith, Klondike Kate, Belinda Mulrooney. For Seattle Public Schools.

CATALOG OF PAULSON DOLLS

Shaped felt heads with a pearl bead placed under the felt for the nose. Felt bodies over wire armatures, padded with surgical cotton. Dolls are three to five inches tall.

1965 *Elves.* (20) Each portrayed at a different activity.

1966 *Elves.* Now sportsmen of many kinds, always with caps pointed to keep elfin look. Hands improved by making one hand with thumb and index finger free, the other with thumb and little finger free.
Angels, Shepherds, and Animals. 9-10" series.
Christopher Robin. 16". With *Pooh* and *Piglet.*
Pollyanna. *Wizard of Oz Characters.* (5)
Mary Poppins. *Pied Piper Characters.* (5)
Hansel and Gretel. *Tom Sawyer and Becky.*
Henners Lydia. *Treasure Island Characters.*
Little House in the Big Woods Characters.
Many nursery rhyme characters.

1967 "Weesemblances." Portraits of Paulson children, *Heidi, Lisa,* and *John;* children of neighbors and friends. Grown-up "Semblances" of cheerleaders, professors, doctors, brides and grooms, etc.

1968 "Weedidits." Some subjects duplicated, but not identically.
Birthday Party Group. *Cheerleader.*
Girl with Checked Apron. *Violet Peddler.*
Snoopy. *Charlie Brown.*
Daisy Girl. *Mailbox Girl.*
Girl with Mirror. *Ann of Green Gables.*
Brother Juniper. *Barefoot Girl with Cat.*
Hot Cross Bun Peddler. *Bus Stop Girl.*
Umbrella Girl. *Friends.*
Thomas and his Gerbil. *Girl on Park Bench.*
Girl with Hatbox and Cat. *Girl with Cradle and Baby.*

The Haircut.
Johnny Mouse.
Chi Omega Pledge.
Blow Your Nose.
Girl Wrapping Packages.
Girl in Swing in Apple Tree.
Paul Bunyan and Babe. 24". (2 pair)
Girl with Feet in Tub of Water.
Herb Alpert and the Lonely Bull.
Girl Warming by Potbellied Stove.
Country Doctor with Horse and Carriage.

"Weesemblances."

Ph. D. Student at Desk.
Ann Erdman.
Graduate.
College Girl.
Bokelman Twins.
Jenny in her Horsey Swing.
World Globe with Dog.
Dr. Mueller Trout Fishing.
Jean and Sue Bokelman.
Debbie and Bobbie Ward.
Greg Sanlan.
Marcia and her Cat.
Nieces.
Pat, the Airline Stewardess.
Heidi.
Peter and Goat.
Herta and Roy Under Palm Tree.
Hilma and Ben at Work on their Hobbies.
Mrs. Vogel in her Garden with two Dogs.
Professor von Stephenson with Rolltop Desk.
Mrs. Hall Fishing at Walleye Hole.
Bert DeHate, Ice Hockey Star.
Little Oscar and Housewife with Grocery Cart. 22". Displayed at Madison, Wisconsin, airport in Oscar Mayer showcase.

1969 "Weedidits."
Charlotte's Web Characters.
Red-Haired Twins at Ice Cream Parlor.
Days of the Week. (7)
Months of the Year. (8)
First Convention Lady.
And 10 others.
"Weesemblances."
Kira. 14".
Stan Bokelman.
B. Enderlein's Nieces and Nephews.
Self-Portrait as Child.
And 22 others.

1970 "Weedidits."
Convention Lady of 1970.
Three Attic Scenes.
Four College Girls, 1900-1970.
And 20 others.
"Weesemblances."
Self-Portrait at Work.
And 18 others.

1971 "Weedidits."
The Blue Cap. (5 scenes)
Convention Lady of 1971.
And 21 others.

"Weesemblances." (14)

1972 "Weedidits."

Convention Lady of 1972.

Social Cohesion. (3 scenes)

Buggy Scenes. (3)

Girl with Umbrella.

Warm Feeling.

Several girls with kittens and boys with dogs.

Note Cards in colors of "Red Loves Hattie," "Warm Feeling," "Follow the Star," "Here!," and "Happy Hanukkah" have been published, 1972-73.

1973 "Weedidits."(32)

Large Farm Scene.

Buggy Scenes. (3)

Corner of Barn.

Girls and Kittens.

Boys and Dogs.

Attic Scene.

Bride and Groom.

Girls in Rockers with Dolls.

Boy on Wall.

Animals. (8)

Convention Lady of 1973.

"Weesemblances."

Harold Gray.

Janet.

Bragdon Children.

Kathy Althen.

Bernie Kaufmann.

Office. With 20 NIADA miniatures.

And 5 others.

CATALOG OF FORSTER DOLLS

All dolls are one-of-a-kind. "Herta Forster" printed on cloth labels are sewn into the costume of each.

1962 *Symphony Conductor.* 14". Very arrogant face.

Franciscan Monk. 14". Fat, pointing to heaven, Bible under arm.

Demimondaine. 14". Jewelry, black umbrella, dog on leash.

Spanish Dancers. Woman 14", man 11" kneeling. Hard faces.

Portrait of my Husband. 11" sitting.

1963 *Old-Fashioned Tailor.* 14". Crosslegged on table, garb ca. 1870.

Carpenter. 14". Ill-humored, sawing lumber. Tools not self-made.

Self-Portrait. 14". In gardening outfit, bad features exaggerated.

African Savage. 14". TWA bag in one hand, dried shriveled head and spear in other hand (abducted traveler). Felt body, anatomically complete.

Apache Dancers. 14". Hard faces, she is a "Left Bank" girl.

1964 *Old Bavarian Peasant.* 14". Friendly bearded face, cane, pipe.

Man with Candle. 14". In long old-fashioned nightgown with black poodle trying to pull tasseled nightcap off his head.

Pirate with Parrot. 14". Typical pirate garb.

Painter. 14". With easel, viewing work. Rembrandt-type clothes.

English Fox Hunter. 19". Pink hunting jacket, appears apprehensive of falling off papier mache horse.

1965 *Beach "Girl".* 14". Early middle-aged, portly beauty in bathing suit.
Rococo Pianist. 10". Condescending, suave. Piano by Ideal Toy Co.
Opera Singer. 14". Stout lady in snobbish theatrical pose.
Mary and Joseph. 14". Part of creche group of eight.
Black King. 14". Part of creche.
Drunk Mermaid. 7". Lying in abalone shell.
Scottish Girl. 16".
American Negro Girl. 16".
Chinese Boy. 14".

1966 *Asian King.* 14". Part of creche.
Old Bavarian Peasant. 11" sitting on stool. Friendly toothless face. Beer mug and cigar.
Old Woman with Baby. 11" sitting. Chair made by Herta Forster. Trying to feed crying baby who holds tiny teddy bear. Dress ca. 1890.
Rococo Lady. 14". Self-important expression.
Centaur. 17". Trying to hit fly on his rear. Part of horse of papier mache. Garlands of flowers around head and waist.
Cook. 14". Tasting food.
Mandarin. 14".
Beetle. 14". Boy with guitar and beetle haircut.
Skier. 14". Skies and one boot on shoulder. One leg in cast.
Christmas Carol Fiddler. 14". Violin. Grouped with flutist and singer.
Shepherd. 14". Part of creche. Lamb in arm.
Woman with Curlers. 12". Fat lady, sitting and holding mirror, yawning. See-through gown.

1967 *Biedermeier Lady.* 20". Dress ca. 1830. Very haughty expression.
President Johnson. 14". Hat in hand, reaching to shake hands.
Biedermeier Man. 18". Top hat in hand, gentle sweet face, ca. 1835.
Genie Rising from Lamp. 14". Arrogant face, arms folded, jewelry.
Lady with Harlequin Dane. 14". Trying to restrain dog made by H.F.
Fisherman with Large Shark. 14". Looking wildly surprised at his catch.
Middle-Aged Surfer. 14". Surfboard, goggles, flippers, etc., all made by H.F.
Puppeteer. 14". Gentle smile, 1850 peasant. Holding clown marionette.
Man Singing in Bathtub. 8". Smiling face. Naked but covered with angel hair "water."
Lady of a Medieval Castle. 14". ca. 1460. Elaborate. Overbearing posture.
Sioux Indian Girl. 16".
Dutch Girl and Boy. 16".
Bolivian Girl. 16". Baby on back.
Bolivian Boy. 16".

American Negro Boy. 16".
Danish Girl and Boy. 16".
Bavarian Boy. 16".
Black Forest Girl and Boy. 16".
Little Old Lady Drinking Coffee. 10" sitting. In rocking chair. Keen, sweet expression.
Clown. 14".
Gentleman in Restoration Garb. 18". Fat, ugly, self-satisfied expression.
Queen. 18". Plump, ugly, domineering. Inspired by "Queen of Hearts."
Cleaning Woman. 14". Drab, sour. Looking for a victim for her mop.
English Bobby. 14". Long, thin, in typical traffic stance.
Witch. 14". Typical fairy-tale witch. Black cat on shoulder.
Little Old Lady in Rocker. 10"sitting. 1850 dress. Knitting. Sweet smile.
Christmas Flutist. 14". One of a group of three.

1968 *Flower Vendor.* 18". Not pretty but genteel. Offering her wares.
Hippie. 14". Guitar and beads.
Dancing Pair. 14". ca. 1880. Obviously two people in love.
Old Man in Reclining Chair. 8". Sleeping with smile on face and a "girly" magazine in his hand. In robe and slippers.
Shepherd. 12". Part of creche. Sitting on a rock, lamb at his feet.
Italian Bird Vendor. 14". 1880 peasant dress. Two bird cages.
Woman with Baby in Highchair. 18". ca. 1890. Baby crying to be fed.
English Pedlar Woman. 12" sitting. Bonnet, cape, and basket of goodies.

1969 *Christmas Singer.* 14". Full, cheerful face. One of a group of three.
Washerwoman. 16". Ugly, coarse. Looking to smack someone with laundry.
Lady in Fur Cape. 14". ca. 1917. Society type, lorgnette, snobbish.
Drunk. 14". Tippler standing on one leg and hoisting another glass.
Hillbilly. 14". Leaning against tree with a jug marked "Four Noses."
Gladys and Tyrone. (Buzzi and Johnson) 11" sitting. On a bench as in "dirty old man" skit. Sold to Ruth Buzzi.
Man at Desk with Canary. 10" sitting. ca. 1825. Sweet, coy face. Bird on hand. Accessories and furniture by H.F.
Old Bob. 14". Old peasant used in illustrating children's story. Three heads to suit various moods.
Mrs. Hag. 14". Two heads, happy and angry, for illustrating story.

1970 *Old Lady with Bird.* 14". "My, what a beak!" Similar profiles.
Bacchus on Donkey. 14". Laurel wreath and lyre. Lifting glass. Papier mache donkey.
Hypochondriac. 13" sitting. In elegant Louis XIV chair by H.F.; pills.

Storybook Character. 14". ca. 1850. Three interchangeable heads.
Little Poet. 10" sitting. ca. 1830. Friendly old man with glasses, sitting at desk. Miniature verses from "Wilhelm Busch."
American Girl and Boy. 16".
Bavarian Girl. 16".

1971 *Vegetable Vendor.* 11" sitting. ca. 1890. Friendly face, wares by H.F.
Victorian Lady. 14". Goodlooking, sophisticated, holding umbrella.
Mark Twain. 10" in rocker.
Man with Loooong Nose. 14". ca. 1850. Three heads, for storybook illustration.
Pink Crinoline Lady. 14". ca. 1840. Sweet face but not pretty.
Doll Collector. 14". ca. 1880. Looking at two prospective buys.
Man with Crystal Ball. 14". ca. 1870. Soothsayer with gentle face trying to look into the future. Influenced by German painter Carl Spitzweg.
Lady in Lavender. 14". Very pretty young woman.
Little Friendly Old Woman. 9" in chair. White poodle beside her.
Old Man. 9". Almost bald. Friendly character.
Little Girl. 13". Head of molded plastic wood, covered with felt. Jointed at neck, legs, and arms. Made in various hair and costume styles.
Little Boy. 13". Same construction and variations in finishing as above.
Surprise. 14". Old lady hanging laundry. Bird perched on long johns.

1972 *Felt Baby.* 13". Dressed in jacket, diaper, and booties.
Friends. 11" sitting. Old man in rocker, petting dog. Pipe.
Empire Lady. 11" sitting. Doing needlework on period sofa with cat on lap.
Gentle Old Man. 11" sitting. Reading paper in rocker. Glasses and pipe.
Late Love. 11" sitting. Old girl writing love letters at desk.

1973 *Love Letters.* 11" sitting. Good-looking middle-aged woman reading a letter at desk with a bemused expression.
Justitia. 12". Justice with scale out of balance. On base she is peeking, unbelieving, from under her blindfold.
Pretty, Old Girl. 11" sitting. At table with stereoscope.
Gentle Grandma. 11" sitting. Mending teddy bear.
Too Nosy. 14". Surprised gent taking baby bird out of birdhouse while father bird is pecking him on bald head.
Mischief. 11" sitting on pilings. Fisherman mending net looks angrily at small dog pulling at end.
Rainy Weather. 18". Coarse old woman with umbrella, looking disgusted.
Feeding Fish. Thin old gent in robe feeding carp, cat watching.
Beautiful Hair. 11" sitting at desk.

Old Man Cactus. Sitting at desk. Long white hair.
1974 *Old Puritan Lady.* Sitting on chair sewing patchwork quilt.

CATALOG OF CAMPBELL DOLLS

Head, hands, and usually feet are porcelain and the jointed bodies are either porcelain, felt, or kid; unless otherwise specified.

1966 *Fashion Doll.* 20". Bisque shoulder head, lower arms, and legs; body, upper arms, and legs are kid. Movable joints, human hair wig woven by the artist or Dynel wig. Current fashions. Limit–50. Discontinued.

1967 *Becky.* 9". Bisque head and arms on felt body with movable felt legs. Dynel wig. Imported Swiss embroidery dress, 1950 style. Limit–100. Discontinued.

1968 *Ricky.* 9". Arms and body identical to *Becky,* boy's head. Velveteen rompers, Dynel wig. Limit–100. Discontinued.

1969 *Alice in Wonderland.* 10". Fully jointed, all bisque, Dynel wig. Bewildered expression. Limit–100. Discontinued.

1971 *Baby Lisa.* 9". Four-month-old baby, all bisque, fully jointed. Hair and features china painted. First version dressed by the artist, later ones undressed. Limited.

1972 *Pioneer Lady.* 11". (1) All bisque upper torso, movable bisque arms, molded hair, made as a candy box. Conceived as a young woman who, though a pioneer, still maintains feminine ways. Timeless expression of hope, patience, and love.

Wax Lady. 22". (1) Head, torso, and lower limbs of wax; body and upper legs of kid. Jointed, glass eyes, and human hair eyebrows and wig, both inserted into head. Ante-bellum silk lace gown.

CATALOG OF STAFFORD DOLLS

1966 *Ada Lou.* 22½" and smaller. (4 or 5) Portrait of mother.

Little Ruthie. 19". (2) Portrait of sister-in-law. High button shoes.

Master Edward. 20½". (4) Portrait of young boy. Fancy suit.

Mary. 20". (10) Portrait of great-aunt as young girl. Eyelet dress.

Huggins and Muggins. 17". (5 sets) First dome head. Boy in blue shorts, girl in pink ruffles. Inspired by baby food ad in magazine.

Twins. 15". (2 sets) Same doll reduced. Dressed for wedding.

Amber. 15". (2) Portrait of neighbor baby. All bisque arms, bent.

Dulcy. 26". (3) Bride doll. Also as fashion lady, 1890 and Fairy Queen.

Pavlova. 16". (1) Toddler as ballet dancer, unusual molded tongue.

Wee Willie Winkie. 16". (1) Little boy in night shirt, open mouth.

1967 *W.S. Hart.* 24". (3) Portrait of movie star. Boots, gloves, and gun belt.

Jackie Coogan. 20". (5) Portrait as "The Kid." Tattered clothes.

Flower Child. 5". (16) All bisque little girl with movable arms.
1968 *Sleepy Baby.* 16". (1) Baby with eyes closed and pouty expression.
1969 *Negro Toddler.* 5". (12) All bisque little girl, molded hair, movable arms.
Estrellita. 20". (3) Mexican girl in authentic print. Bisque legs.
Sue Ling. 18". (10) Korean toddler in red satin and gold velvet.
Angelique. 15". (10) Two-faced toddler, sleepy or wide awake; bonnet.
1970 *Annabelle Lee.* 4". (10) Baby, bisque arms and legs.
Mary Pickford. 22". (5) Portrait of old-time movie star as "Little Mary."
Peaches. 16". (10) Baby doll with innocent expression and cry box.
Merry Christmas Carol. 15". First in a series of Christmas dolls.
Marsha. 18". (2) Portrait doll, open-closed mouth, molded teeth.
1971 *Primm Family.* (12 sets) All bisque arms and legs. Includes baby Primrose, twins Perry and Polly, papa Pembrook, and mother Prudence.
Grace. 12". (10) Gibson Girl. Fashion type with molded bust and shoes.
Buttercup. 15". (10) Negro toddler, bisque arms and legs, yellow dress.
1972 *April.* 6". (75) All bisque jointed baby. First in a series of calendar dolls.
May. 6". (35) Black baby with bent legs.
Becky. 15". (10) Little girl with long blonde wig, bisque legs.
Sonja Henie. (1) Portrait of movie and skating star, all bisque, jointed.
Nelson Eddy. (1) Portrait of star, all bisque, costume from "Maytime."
Jeanette MacDonald. 16". (1) Portrait of star, costume from "Maytime.
1973 *June.* 6". (35) Oriental girl, all bisque, jointed, orange dress.
July. 6". (35) Little boy, all bisque, jointed, blue and white suit.
Birdie. 13". (15) Baby, cloth body, blue glass eyes, blonde hair.

Catalog of Gibson Dolls

1935 *Wooden Dolls.*
1959 *Ceramic Dolls.* With kid bodies.
Cloth-Sculptured Dolls.
1960 *Porcelain Dolls.* Exclusively porcelain after this date. Various combinations.
Little Charlotte. Portrait of the artist's mother as a little girl.
1961 *Little Girls.* 10-18". Made for I. Magnin.
1965 *Fashion Dolls.* 15-23". Head, upper torso, arms, and lower legs porcelain; cloth body.

Nannies. 23". Head, upper torso, arms, and lower legs porcelain; arms jointed at elbow and wrist; cloth body.

1966 *Baby Dolls.* Head and hands porcelain; cloth body.

Gentlemen. 17-25". Five sizes. Head and limbs porcelain. Mates for fashion ladies.

Portraits.

1967 *Twiggy.*

1968 *Ballerinas.* 19". Head, upper torso, arms, and legs porcelain; fully jointed or straight arms and legs; cloth bodies.

1969 *Peter.* All porcelain.

Blanche Woolsey. Portrait.

Pas de Quatre. 19". Group of four ballerinas.

1971 *Ruth Shurtleff.* Portrait.

1972 *Godey Ladies.* Head, upper torso, arms, and lower legs porcelain; cloth body.

Gibson Girls. 18-20". Similar construction as above.

Boy Doll. Porcelain head and limbs, cloth body.

1973 *Taglioni Ballerina.* 19". White glazed porcelain shoulder head, arms, and legs; cloth torso.

Kalico Kids. 18". Four girls and one boy. Porcelain shoulder heads, lower arms, and legs; cloth body.

Catalog of Saucier Dolls

Hardened felt technique, felt over composition, painted features; usually swivel necks and hip joints, wired fingers, Saran wigs; unless otherwise noted. Most are copyrighted and registered as works of art. Limited quantities.

1945 *Baby Doll.* (1) Needle-sculptured features on fabric, articulated limbs. Five-year-old.

Girl. 10". (4) First communion dress. White.

Children. 10". (20) Mostly nineteenth century costumes.

1952 *Nativity Group.* (3 sets)

Christ Child as Bambino. (1)

Scottish Girl. 10". Annie Laurie period.

1962 *First Canadian Series.* 12-14". (40) Commissioned by Robert Simpson and Company, Toronto.

Red River Girl. 12". (1) With snowshoes.

Madeleine de Vercheres. 14". (45)

Habitant Woman. 14". (50) 1806 costume, with straw basket.

1963 *National Costume Dolls.* 12-14". (2 sets) A group of seventeen in various national costumes, commissioned by the Fashion Group of America. Reproduced in 1966 for Jordan Marsh, Boston.

1964 *Canadian Marine Officers.* 14". (40) Various ranks, drummers, flag bearers, etc., of the Compagnies Franches de la Marine.

1965 *Canteen Girls.* 12-14". (10) Girls of the above regiments.

Mrs. John Graves Simcoe. 14". (21)

Little Girls in their Sunday Best. 12". (17)
Helene Boulle de Champlain. 14".
Farmer Boy. 12". (12)
Suzanne. 14½". (2) Portrait of a three-year-old girl wearing father's top hat.
Suzanne. 14½". (2) Portrait of a four-year-old girl, representing the Providence of Quebec, holding emblematic lilies.
Pierre. 16½". (2) Portrait. Costumed as the Canadian Beaver.
John C. 17". Portrait of a six-month-old boy as Canadian Snow Baby.
Femme du Quebec. 24". (3) From the Grevedon lithograph, ca. 1851. Her two brooches were reproduced by Montreal branch of Van Cleef and Arpels, jewelers.
Samuel de Champlain. 19". (9) "Father of New France."
Helene Boulle de Champlain. 17½". (5) Young wife of above.
The Voyageur. 19". (1) In his city clothes.
Royal Canadian Mounted Policeman. 19". (6)
*Pierrette.*16½". (4) Dressed in Red River costume.
Lili. 16½". (9) Inspired by a Renoir but dressed in pants suit.
1968 *1730 Couple.* Man 29", woman 24". In sable and mink.
1968 Couple. Man 29", woman 24". In lamb and black diamond mink.

Both couples were commissioned by a Montreal fur designer who makes furs for Queen Elizabeth II, the Dowager Queen, and the Royal ladies.

1972 *Fanchon.* 14½". (6) Auburn hair. Dressed in 1865 period.

Catalog of Bell Dolls

Porcelain head and hands in various shades of colored porcelain, painted features, and sawdust-stuffed cloth bodies. Copyrighted, with doll's name and "Bertabell," her trade name, incised above copyright mark. On one leg is a label with character's name and on each is a tag with a thumbnail sketch. Dolls are sixteen to eighteen inches tall.

1969 *George Washington Carver.* (78) In lab apron. Eminent scientist known as the "Savior of Southern Agriculture" and the "Peanut Wizard."
Mary McLeod Bethune. (82) Famous educator, humanitarian, and advisor to President Franklin Roosevelt.
Harriet Tubman. (60) Known as "The Moses of her People," she led over three hundred slaves to freedom during nineteen journeys to the South.
Sojourner Truth. (58) Abolitionist-suffragette. Born in slavery and when freed, felt it her duty to "sojourn up and down the land and tell the truth about the evils of slavery." Changed her name from Isabella Baumfree to "Sojourner Truth."

Paul Laurence Dunbar. (25) Known as "The Poet of the People," he wrote both in conventional English and in the various Negro dialects.

Crispus Attucks. (18) Patriot-martyr of the Revolutionary War, he was the first to die in Boston Commons in defense of American liberty.

1971 *Jean Baptiste Point de Sable.* (14) First citizen of Chicago, Illinois. A wealthy trapper and fur trader, he married a Potawatomi Indian.

W.C. Handy. (20) "The Father of the Blues." Famous for "St. Louis Blues," "Memphis Blues," and "Beale Street Blues." Wrote many oratorios and serious music as well.

Dr. Daniel Hale Williams. (15) The first open heart surgeon. The Chicago Tribune in 1893 carried this headline about him, "SEWED UP HIS HEART." Founder of Provident Hospital and Nurses' School.

1972 *Frederick Douglass.* (12) Abolitionist-orator, newspaper editor, United States Recorder of Deeds, and Minister to Haiti for the United States.

Anna Murray Douglass. (10) Wife of Frederick Douglass, she aided him financially and with moral support, in his escape from slavery.

Solon C. Bell. (12) Labor leader. Founder of the first union among dining car employees on the Union Pacific Railroad in the 1930s.

Ashanti Queen Mother. (8) Representing queen from Ashanti (Ghana), a section of Africa from which most of the African slaves came. She could easily have been the ancestor of any contemporary Black Americans. Costumed with much gold jewelry and gold trim.

Matthew Henson. (10) Accompanied Admiral Peary in expeditions designed to discover the North Pole. When the pole was reached, on April 6, 1908, Peary handed the United States flag to Henson, who placed it at the pole. They were the first to reach the North Pole.

Amos Fortune. (9) Born a prince in Africa, he was kidnapped and sold into slavery in America. According to the epitaph on his tombstone in Jaffrey, New Hampshire, "purchased liberty, professed Christianity, lived reputably, and died hopefully, Nov. 17, 1801, at the age of ninety-one."

1973 *George Glenn.* (12) Black cowboy who rode the Chisholm Trail from Abilene, Kansas, to San Antonio, Texas.

James Beckwourth. One of the famous "mountain men." Explorer, guide, and teller of tall tales. He is credited with putting Reno, Nevada, on the map by discovering the lowest point across the Sierra Nevada Mountains. It became a favorite route settlers used to get to the Northwest.

Oliver Lewis. (8) A black jockey who rode Aristides to win the first Kentucky Derby in 1875.

Dr. W.E.B. DuBois. (5) One of the greatest scholars of all time; he received a Ph.D. from Harvard University, studied at the University of Berlin, became one of the founders of the NAACP, and has been listed in WHO'S WHO IN AMERICA since its first publication.

1974 *Prince Hall.* (5) A black pioneer abolitionist in Massachusetts, a minister in the Methodist church, he organized the first black Masons, and was a member of the Continental Army. He influenced the Massachusetts State Legislature to provide free school facilities to all.

Benjamin Banneker. (5) Mathematical wizard and inventor. He published an almanac in 1791, made the first clock wholly made in America, and helped to survey and layout the streets of Washington, D.C.

Elizabeth Keckley. (10) Dressmaker, friend, and confidante to Mary Todd Lincoln.

Catalog of Sullo Dolls

Self-hardening clay on heavy wire armature, body then wrapped with strips of cotton. "Sullo" and year incised on back of head. All dolls are one-of-a-kind. Approximate size is twelve inches.

1940	*Japanese Girl.*	*Indian Girl.*
	American Girl.	
1941	*Spanish Man and Girl.*	*Italian Girl.*
1942	*Colonial Boy and Girl.*	
1943	*Gay Nineties Matron.*	*Monk.*
1946	*Jordanoff Portrait Doll.*	
1948	*Padula Portrait Doll.*	*Pasco Portrait Doll.*
1951	*Milano Wedding Party.*	
1952	*Gay Nineties Bride.*	
1957	*Organ-Grinder with Monkey and Music Box.* (2 sets)	
	Grandma.	
1958	*Grandpa.*	*Orchestra Conductor.*
	German Butcher.	*Blacksmith.*
1959	*Keystone Cop.* (2)	
1960	*Singing Waiters.* (Group of 4) Gay Nineties.	
1961	*Baseball Trio.* Depicting "Casey Striking Out."	
1962	*Balloon Man.*	
	Mudgutter Band. (Group of 3) Playing trombone, tuba, and cornet.	
1963	*The Duffer.* (2)	*The Hunter.*
	The Fisherman. (After A.B. Frost.)	
1971	*Kaufmann Portrait Doll.*	*Barlebough Portrait Doll.*
	The Doughboy of 1918.	*"I Cash Clothes" Man.*

President William H. Taft as a Golfer.
1972 *We Came in Peace for all Mankind.* President Nixon and Chairman Mao.
1973 *Pedlar.* *Country Fiddler.* Portrait doll.
Hobo King. *Estate Gardener.* Portrait doll.
Homemaker's Delight. Portrait of Joe Genovese, furniture maker.
The Truthfinder. Portrait of Senator Sam Irvin.
1974 *Wee Paulson Portrait.* *Jake Jacobson Portrait.*

CATALOG OF CONDON DOLLS

Porcelain head, hands, and usually lower legs. Usually jointed at shoulders and hips. Glass eyes and wigs. Cloth-covered, stuffed body with wire armature. Exceptions as noted.

1955 *Russian Ballet Dancers.* 23". (1 male, 1 female) Heads of plastic wood.
1971 *Alistair.* 42". (1) English barrister. Wax-covered papier mache head, body papier mache over wire armature.
Rosey the Witch. 42". (1) Wax over papier mache head, body papier mache over wire armature, hands molded of rubber.
St. George and the Dragon. 45". (1 set) Wax-covered papier mache head, body papier mache over wire armature, plastic eyes.
Ann and Gertrude. 28". Gibson Girls. Porcelain. Elbows and knees jointed also.
Frankie. 8". (13) Black porcelain. Shoulder head.
Michael. 14". (13) Porcelain shoulder head.
Hugo. 19". (1) Court Jester. Shoulder head. Elbows and knees jointed also.
Belinda. 21". (8) Black porcelain. Shoulder head.
1972 *Sanford.* 18½". (1) Dance choreographer. Shoulder head. Elbows and knees jointed also. Molded hair.
Lena and Leroy. 10½" and 8½". (1 pair) Black porcelain. Neck and elbows jointed also. They hold hands.
Paul. 15". (1) Black porcelain. Neck, elbows, and knees jointed also.
Karan. 8½". (1) Ballet dancer. Elbows, waist, and knees jointed also.
Kathy, Becky, and Laura. 11½". Porcelain. Elbows, wrists, knees, and ankles jointed also.
Hilda and Vickie. 12". Porcelain. Neck, elbows, wrists, waist, knees, and ankles jointed also.
1973 *Louisa and Lelia.* 18½". Porcelain. Neck, elbows, and knees jointed also.
Ronda. 11". Porcelain. Elbows, knees, and neck jointed also.
Charles. 12". Porcelain. Neck, elbows, and knees jointed also.
Zeke. 20". Karate clown. Porcelain. Elbows, shoulders, and knees jointed also.

Catalog of Deutsch Dolls

Heads of latex composition, after 1969 some in plaster, covered with stretched chamois and oil painted. Bodies heavily wired, wrapped, padded, and covered with stretch jersey. Exceptions as noted. All stand firmly without base. Signed.

1960 *Santa Claus.* 18". (4) 20", 30", and 40". (2 each) Papier mache face covered in chamois and oil painted. Three eighteen-inch dolls are in gold satin; one in pink satin.

Madonna. 18". (4) 21". (2) 30". (9) Lame or velvet. Some seated.

Gnome with Grapes. 15". (1) Velvet leaves and grapes.

Adoration Group. 21". (2 sets) Six characters, six animals, two palms.

1961 *Pink Angel.* 30". (1) Original in pink and gold organza. 18-30". (7) White and gold organza.

Holy Family. 20". (1 set) 18-21". (4 sets) Mary, Joseph, and Babe.

Nativity Scene. 21". (13 sets) Eight characters, eight animals, four props.

1962 *Carol Singers.* 19". (4 sets) Girl singer, boy with French horn, and man with bass.

Old-Fashioned Couple. 19". (1 couple) 21" and 24". (4 couples) In brocade and wool.

Bride. 30". (1) White satin, lace applique, beading.

Romeo and Juliet. 30". (1 pair) Romeo in gold; Juliet, pink with pearl cap.

1963 *Minuet Dancers.* 19". (2 pairs) Colonial period, brocades and velvets.

Colonial Couple. 27". (2 couples) In brocades and velvets.

Godey Fashion Lady and Gentleman. 19". (10 couples) In velvet, taffeta, and wool.

1880 Pink Lady. 30". (4) Pink brocade and lace, flower bonnet.

1964 *Daniel Boone.* 27". (3) Mocassins, rifle, and buckskins.

Organ Grinder and Monkey. 24". (1 set) Corduroy pants, wool coat, and scarf.

Pioneer Family. 24". (2 sets) Early western man and woman with baby. One in 1966 with small boy added.

Grandmother in Chair. 24". (2) Dark dress, lace fissue, knitting.

Girl with Doll. 12". (17) Late 1800 style.

Boy with Dog. 13". (2) Late 1800 style.

Boy. 13". (20) Late 1800 style. Seventeen with hoop; two with toy; one with dog.

Square Dancers. 18". (1 pair) Man western style; girl full skirt.

1965 *Southern Belle and Beau.* 30". (3 pairs) Girl in flowered sheer; man, formal.

Scarlett O'Hara and Rhett Butler. 25" and 27". (1 pair)

1966 *Christmas Shoppers.* 30". (1 pair) Man in top hat; woman, velvet coat.

Boy with Stick Horse. 14". (2) Brown wool suit.
Pioneer Girl. (2) With flower basket and doll. Dress, bonnet, and apron.
Haston Children. 6-16". (1 set) Early 1900 portraits. Three girls and one boy.
The Texan. 19". (1) Western hat, shirt, boots, etc.
Abraham Lincoln. 18". (1) 22". (2) As president. Black suit, top hat, and boots.
Brackney Boy. 19". (1) Portrait. In Rhett Butler costume.

1967 *Boy Fisherman.* 12½". (2) Early 1900. Straw hat and fishpole.
Pioneer Boy. 12½". (4)
Girl in Pink with Doll. 12". (1)
Boy with Goose. 12½". (1) From Pioneer Group.

1968 *Pic-nic Girl.* 17". (1) Large white hat, white dress, basket.
Godey Fashion Lady. 18". (5) Two standing, three sitting.
Girl with Hoop. 12". (3) From Renoir painting.
Girl from Dickens. 15". (2) With songbook and violin.
Boy of 1800s. 12½". (1)
Girl of 1800s. 12". (1) Figured taffeta.
Bride of 1860. 19". (1) From Godey print.
Boy on Rocking Horse. 18". (2) Blue velvet, high hat, sword.
Boy and Dog, Girl and Kitten. 13" and 12". (1 pair) From old color print.

1969 *Christmas Girl.* 12½". (1) From an old German print. Packages and doll.
Christmas Boy. 13½". (1) From an old German print. Pulls sled with boxes and tree.
Pinafore Miss. 12½". (1) Alice in Wonderland style. Carries doll.

1970 *Brown Eyes.* 14". (1) From an old German print. Little boy with velvet suit.
Blue Eyes. 13". (1) From an old German print. Girl with blue velvet coat, white hat, and muff.
Young George Washington. 14". (1) Breeches, tricon, holds hatchet.
Boy with Wagon. 13". (1) Early 1900 boy in overalls.

1971 *Early American Children.* (1 set) From story books. With their farm friends. Set includes:
Israel Boone. 14". With Hannibal, his goose.
Lisa. 14". With rake and hay.
Katy. 7". Sitting on hay and holding white kitten.
Bessie. 14". Holding basket of fruit.
Boy Fisherman. 14". With pole, worms, and shaggy dog.
Background has one cow and three sheep.

1973 *Nativity Scene.* 21". (1 set) 1961 scene expanded to fourty-seven pieces: Joseph, Mary, Jesus, three Kings, six shepherds, twenty sheep, three camels, one ox, one donkey, a shed, jeweled star, and eight palms.

Catalog of Robinson Dolls

All porcelain parts, unless otherwise specified, marked "Pat Robinson," date, and ©.

1964 *John F. Kennedy.* Man and woman. All sculptured cloth.
Cleopatra. 8¼". All ceramic, jointed.
Anthony. 9". All ceramic, jointed.

1965 *John F. Kennedy.* 30½". Ceramic shoulder head, hands, and feet; sawdust-stuffed cloth body.
Mona Lisa. 28". Ceramic shoulder head, hands, and feet, stuffed body.
Statue of Liberty. 26". All wood, jointed.

1966 *Clark Gable.* 18". Porcelain shoulder head, hands, and feet.
Jackie Kennedy. 28". Porcelain upper torso, jointed arms, and legs.
Dean Martin. 32". Hydrastone swivel head and hands.
Getsya. 16". Two-faced, all-wood child.
Lincoln. 19". Wax head and hands; wrapped wire body. Hair set in head.
Marcia. 22". Poured wax shoulder head and lower arms. Exhibited at Expo '67 in Montreal.

1967 *Newborn Baby.* 9". Wood and plastic-wood combination
Fashion Lady of 1830. 18". Papier mache shoulder head, lower arms, and legs; cotton-stuffed body.
Man of 1850. 17". Porcelain shoulder head and hands.
Fashion Lady of 1820. 17½". Poured wax shoulder head, lower arms, and legs.

1970 *Theresa Tonty.* 14½". First white child born in Detroit (1702). Porcelain shoulder head, arms, and lower legs; cotton body, sawdust stuffed.

1971 *Engelbert Humperdinck.* 21". Porcelain shoulder head and hands.
Tom Jones. 20½". Porcelain shoulder head and hands; wire frame body, cotton wrapped.

1972 *Engelbert Humperdinck.* 12". All porcelain, jointed.
Tom Jones. 12". All porcelain, jointed.
Getsya. 13". (Tearful) All porcelain toddler.
Getsya. 13". (Pleased) All porcelain toddler.

1973 *Self-Portrait.* 15". All porcelain, jointed.
Engelbert Humperdinck. 17". All porcelain, jointed.
Tom Jones. 17". All porcelain, jointed.

Catalog of Barrie Dolls

Torsos and heads on the twelve-inch dolls are layers of cotton, butter muslin, and fine paper soaked in glue and applied over a sculptured form, which is made of low-fired clay. The laminated material is pressed into the desired contours and allowed to dry. Legs and arms are of felt over padded wires;

thumbs are separate. Exceptions as noted. Each doll is signed and numbered on the back of the body.

1955-56 *Soft Toys.*

1957 *Scottish Women.* 15". In occupational costumes. Playdolls made for Scottish Craft Centre, Fort William, Scotland.

Rob Roy MacGregor. 15". (1) 12". (39) The fifteen-inch doll was made for the Handcraft Exhibit of the National Association of Townswomen's Guilds at Olympia, England.

1967 *Anna of Romania.* 12". (1) Married spinner with distaff and drop spindle in costume of Banat district. Three in earlier costume.

Maria of Poltava, Ukraine. 12". (4) Unmarried girl in festival dress with basket of decorated Easter eggs.

Katrina of Kurpie, Poland. 12". (2) Carries flower wreath with candles for midsummer festival.

Mistress Bronwen, Cardigan, West Wales. 12". (31) Middle-aged woman in national dress, about 1790. Wool clothes, hand woven.

1969 *Beau Charlie.* 16". English gentleman, 1665. Black silk and velvet clothes. All felt with head sculptured instead of molded.

Mother and Child. 12". (1 pair) Newhaven, Scotland, fishwife and daughter on base representing jetty. Mother sells fish, daughter makes daisy chain.

Mhairi Robertson. 12". (14) Scottish woman in hand-woven tartan carrying creel of peat on her back.

Padraich. 11". (4) Irish peatcutter with slane (barrow) of County Antrim type and peatcutting tool.

1970 *Old Tex.* 12". (7) Texas cowboy of the 1860s, complete with chaps, Texas spurs, gun belt with bullets, and gun in holster (all handmade).

1971 *Elizabeth I.* 15". (1) All felt with sculptured face. Costume taken from the Hardwick portrait with embroidered petticoat.

Jamie McLachlan. 12". (1) Commissioned portrait. Scot in McLachlan tartan, hand woven to scale, carrying sword and leather-covered, studded targe or shield. Black hair and beard.

1973 *Merchant Morgan.* 12". (9) Husband of Mistress Bronwen, in 1790 costume, carrying umbrella and gold watch with fob.

Mary, Queen of Scots. 12". Morton portrait of 1580. Copied from the original in Kelingrove Galleries, Glasgow. Limit–15.

Robert the Bruce. 18". Scottish King and soldier. Thirteenth and fourteenth centuries. Sculptured felt head; wears both chain and plate mail. Limit–15.

English Nanny. 15". (1) Needle-sculptured head with each hair individually attached. Underclothes 1940, typical "Nanny" uniform.

Baby Jean. 4". (1) To go with carriage and Nanny. Needle-sculptured head, felt body. Wearing British baby clothes of 1940, hand-knit, hand-embroidered.

Courtly Joe. 18". (1) Molded head covered with acrylic to resemble the finish on the comb wooden doll in French court costume of 1804, with which it is paired. Lavishly embroidered court costume.
Bride and Groom Series. 12". (1 pair) Danish, Copenhagen area.
Lithuanian Bride and Groom. 12". (1 pair)
Lithuanian Bride. (1)
1974 *Swedish Bride and Groom.* (4 pairs) Skane district. (Research done at Malmo Museum costume collection in Sweden.)
Joan of Arc. 18". (6) Sculptured head; full armor.
Elizabeth I. 17". (1) From the Hardwick portrait. Sculptured felt head, more elaborately dressed with hand-embroidered petticoats, each garment forming part of a sampler of Elizabethan embroidery.
The Star Spangled Banner. (1) First of the "Stars and Stripes Series" depicting incidents from the development of our national flag. Three figures: Mary Pickersgill, her mother, and her daughter with the flag in the process of construction. Furniture, etc., from examples in Flag House, Baltimore.

Catalog of Johnson Dolls

Porcelain heads, hands, and feet with cloth bodies, unless otherwise specified. All dolls before 1964 one-of-a-kind, no records, but at least one hundred made. Sewn label, "Originals by Sharon."

1964 *Lady Margaret.* 17" and 20". (25 each) Dressed 1900 style.
Cissy. 12". (4 or 5) Young black girl.
Jamaica Washerwoman. 22". (1) Self-hardening clay.
1965 *Tommy and Tammy.* 12". (15 pairs) 16". (6 pairs) Red-haired twins, "poutys" with eyes looking sideways. Contemporary costumes.
Little Bit. 26". (6) Toddler with long curly wig.
Petunia. (6) Same doll as above, as black child. Bare feet, mohair pigtails.
Tancy and Babe. (12 pairs) Young black mother in nightgown with all-porcelain, jointed baby.
Honeybun. 11". Blonde pigtailed little girl, sculptured hair.
Teddy Bear. 15". (2) Same as above, as black girl. Black painted hair.
Traipsin' Woman. 14". (50) Portrait of eighty-six-year-old Jean Thomas at age forty; costumed in usual black dress, white collar, and cuffs.
1966 *Abe Lincoln.* 17". (50) Dark sculptured eyebrows, hair, and beard.
Grandparents. Pa 9½", Ma 8½". (6 pairs) Painted gray molded hair and blue eyes. Both in Sunday best clothes.
Georgia. 10". (15) Character face with one eye slightly crossed.
1967 *Wee Devon.* 16". (3 or 4) 20". (2) Portrait of youngest son, sculptured blond hair.

Tecumseh. 17". (12) Black molded hair, weathered face. Deerskins.

1968 *Baby Dimple.* 10" head circumference. (12) Poured wax on Bye-lo type body. (6) Wax over porcelain. Portrait of daughter at six months. Christening dress.

Miss Pinky. 14". (12) A mulatto of old New Orleans. Warm brown porcelain. Wig, black shiny hair, upswept. Frilly pink dress and hat.

Amy. 15". (2) Bride of 1900s. Molded bust. Wedding gown and veil.

Poteet. 12". (15) Little black girl in French bisque style.

Evelyn. 12". (1) Portrait of two-year-old. Brown human hair wig.

Christy. 15". (19) From CHRISTY, by C. Marshall. Gibson Girl dress.

1969 *Fern.* 11". (12) Two dressed 1910 period; nine ca. 1860; one as Bo Peep.

Katie. 15". (1) Elderly woman in contemporary dress.

1970 *Sugar.* 11". (1) Black toddler in shirt and pants.

1971 *Dorothy.* 15". (1) "Pouty," dark wig, 1910 style dress.

Will and Ruby Mae. 14" and 12". (12 pairs) 1860 "Playmates." Portraits from tintypes. Brown glass eyes; boy curly blond, girl brown wig.

Gladys and Christine. 13" and 11". (12 pairs) 1920 "Playmates." Portraits. White dresses, molded hair, and hair bows.

1973 *Derek and Dimple.* 11" and 9". (12 pairs) "Playmates." Two oldest children as toddlers. All porcelain, jointed. Molded hair, play suits.

Priscilla. 12". (12) All porcelain, jointed. Pouty face, long red curly wig, 1940 dress.

Katie. 14". (25) Gibson Girl. Bosom modeled, red wig, green eyes.

Sarah. 12". (12) A Dunkard grandmother of Southern Ohio "River Brethren." Authentic apron dress, cape, and white cap.

Catalog of Tuttle Dolls

Early dolls pottery clay; after 1954, porcelain. Dollhouse-size, scaled one inch to one foot, making babies two and one-fourth inches and eight-year olds four and one-half inches.

1953 *Little Girl.* 6-1/8". (2) Pottery clay.

1954 *Teena.* 4". (3)

1955 *Later Teena.* 3½". (25) Pink porcelain.

1957 *Rosalie.* 5". (2)

1963 *Janie.* 4½". (14)

1964 *Infanta Margarita Maria.* 3½". (17) From Velasquez painting.

Karen. 4". (19)

1965 *Kevin.* 4". (19)

Tammie. 3½". (16)

Jon. 4½". (1)

Angel Baby. 2¼". (82)

Timmy. 3½". (6)

1966 *Honey Lamb.* 2¼". (9)

Cindy. 3½". (9)

Chucky. 3½". (5) *Candy.* 4". (6)
Chet. 4". (2)
All five black children.
Renny. 4". (1) White boy.

1968 *Don Manuel Osorio.* 4". (9) From Goya painting.

1969 *Infanta Margarita Maria.* 4". (8) From Velasquez painting.
Girl with a Watering Can. 4". (8) From Renoir painting.
Liz. 3½". (2) Black girl.

1970 *Katie Greenaway.* 4". (5) From Greenaway illustrations.
Thomas Greenaway. 4". (1) From Greenaway illustrations.

1971 *Two Charpentier Children.* 3½" and 4". (1 set) From Renoir painting.

1972 *Mary Louisa Boit.* 4½". (1) From Sargent painting.

1973 *Pepito Costa y Bonells.* 4". (1) From Goya painting.

1974 *Colette.* 4". (1)

Catalog of Park Dolls

Heads, hands, and feet wax over unfired ceramic clay, hardened with dextrine; bodies stuffed over wire armature. Dolls in 1973 were wax over porcelain head, hands, and feet. Exceptions as noted. From late 1969 all dolls have printed label, "NIADA, Irma Park" on backs.

1953 *Shadow Box Scenes.* 3-5½" figures. Includes:
Joan of Arc. (1) Kneeling before Madonna who is blessing her sword.
Wynken, Blynken, and Nod. (1 set) Sailing in wooden shoe on sea of dew.
Pied Piper. (1) On wharf, blowing flute, followed by a dozen mice.
Alice in Wonderland. (1) Wooded scene; Alice seated watching Blue Caterpillar with hookah, Mock Turtle, March Hare, Dormouse, Gryphon, and other characters gathered around Pool of Tears.

1953-60 *Kings and Queens.* 6½". (1 set) Twenty-three Kings and twenty-eight Queens. All fifty-one different, from fourteenth to eighteenth centuries.

1957 *Goofy Rube and Silly Sis.* 11½" and 18". Barefoot in country dress. Felt dolls, "limpies" with loose joints.
Limpy Lou. 11½" and 18". Same construction as above. Striped stockings, bowery type.
Limber Lil. 11½" and 18". Also a "limpy," 1900 bathing suit. About fifty made of this 1957 group of four "limpy" dolls.

1961-63 *Pipo the Clown.* 11". (About 14) In kit form. Head, wax-coated cornstarch and salt formula. Wired and cotton-stuffed body ready to assemble. Cut-out material and directions for two suits, Emmett Kelly and regular clown type.
Fat Lady. 11". (2) Eating a roasted chicken.
Fashionable Lady. 11". (1) At bar with cocktail glass.
Baldish Timid Man. 11". (1) Coming to call with candy and flowers.
Pregnant Young Woman. 11". (2) Barefooted woman in sandals,

capris, and maternity blouse. One-year-old child in arms, two-year-old girl dragged along.

Country Girl. 11½". (1) Suitcase, birdcage, umbrella.

Peddler Grannie. 11". (1) ca. 1820. Bonnet and red cloak over figured dress with white apron. Woven tray for trinkets.

1963-69 *Notion Grannie.* (130-140) To Kimport for resale.

1964 *Miniatures.* Adults 2¾", children 2¼". Wax over composition head, hands, and feet; wire base bodies.

Grandma and Grandpa. (5-8 pairs) Standing.

Fat Lady and Fat Man. (5-8 pairs)

Pipo the Clown. (5-8)

Girl of 1890 and Girl of 1910. (5-8)

Fisher Boy. (5-8) Barefoot and freckled.

1965 *Shadow Box Scenes.* 5½-6" figures. Wax over composition. Includes:

Homer. (1) Several men standing and sitting, listening to Homer with his lyre, reciting. Setting is interior of 800 B.C. home.

Joan of Arc. 2¾". (15) Blue with silver armor and flag. (To Kimport)

1966 *Hap.* 2¾". (27) Clown in Emmett Kelly suit. (To Kimport)

Hazard. 2¾". (27) Originally *Pipo,* renamed by Kimport.

Queen Elizabeth I. 3". (15) To Kimport.

Mary, Queen of Scots. 3". (15) To Kimport.

Beginning of the 1" Dolls. Wax over composition on head only; body with wire base. Legs and arms when dressed are size of a round toothpick or smaller. Slip and pantalettes on each girl.

Tom Thumb. 1". (150) Robin Hood-style costume. (To Kimport)

Beginning of the 2¼" Children. Wax over composition heads, arms, and legs; little filled-out bodies. Slips and lace-trimmed panties, mohair or combed yarn wigs. Stationary on base. Label beneath base. Have their own dolls of 1" or smaller.

Broken Doll. 1-5/8". (160) Girl ca. 1860. Crying because her little wooden cart tipped backwards, breaking her 1" doll's head. Red bobbed hair, blue dress, and white pinafore.

Waiting. 1-7/8". (152) Girl ca. 1820. Straw poke bonnet and blue visiting dress, seated in chair with cushion at feet. Holds a 1" doll.

Little Mama. 1-7/8". (160) Girl ca. 1860. Long blonde hair, pinafore over pink dress. Looking down at her 1" doll in a two-wheeled hooded carriage

1967 *Happy Days.* 1-7/8". (3) Fisher boy.

First Love. 1-7/8". (3)

Peddler Grannie. 11". (14) The 1963 model, made with head and hands wax over composition.

Hobo Joe. 2¾". (3)

Artist at Easel. 2¾". (2) Made with *Fat Man's* head.

Grannie in Rocker. 2¾". (15) The 1964 Grannie seated with Bible in high-backed rocker.

Dolly May. 2". (96) Dress ca. 1820. A doll's doll, same type and construction as child, but not on a base.

Girl. 5/8". (10)

Girl. 1-1/8". (11)

Ghost. 1". (12)

Li'lest Peddler. 1". (96) Straw bonnet over mobcap, dress and apron under red cloak. Tray full of trinkets.

Clown. 1". (12)

Clown. 1". (28) On a ball.

Baby Face #1. 7/8". (6)

Baby Face. (41) In cradle.

Fisher Boy. 1". (23) Straw hat and overalls, carries pole.

Thumbelina. 1". (26) In a walnut shell. Blonde yarn hair.

Girl. 1". (13) Straw hat and pink dress.

Baby Features #1. 5/8". (55) Lying on pad.

Doll's Doll #1. 1". (101)

Doll's Doll #2. 1". (66)

Dolly Bess #1. 1". (85) Blonde hair and blue dress.

Girl. 15/16". (91) Straw bonnet.

Boy. 1". (74) Straw hat.

Boy. 7/8". (37) Same design as above.

Humpty Dumpty. 1-3/8". (20) Egg-shaped body with arms and legs wax over composition. Dressed.

1968 *Fairy.* 1". (12) In Easter egg.

Raggedy Ann and Andy. 1". (4 pairs)

Boy and Girl Rabbits. 1¼". (17 sets) Composition head, painted white, pink tint in ears, white flock over back of head and ears; wired body. Dressed, standing. Carrying straw baskets of eggs.

Mouse Family. Papa 1¼". (34) Mama 1¼". (40) Baby 7/8". (38) Composition heads painted brown, brown flock on wired bodies. Dressed.

Mama and Papa Mouse as Bride and Groom. (2 pairs)

Leprechaun. 1". (28) High hat, pointed shoes, knee pants, shirt, and vest.

Baby. (35) In long dress. (38) In short dress. New features.

Little Rags. 1". (36 boys, 46 girls) Black girl with bandana, boy like Golliwog.

Rags Clown. 1". (24)

Dolly Goo. 1¾". (46) A doll's doll with chubby head, arms, and legs.

Lady Doll Maker. 5½". (2) Working on a 2" *Dolly May.*

Baby. 1½". (87) Long dress.

Kiss for Dolly. 1-5/8". (64) ca. 1860. Red bobbed hair, yellow dress, white pinafore. Mouth puckered, holding her ¾" doll to kiss.

Arms Full. 1-7/8". (140) Face same as *Little Mama.* Blonde braids, ca. 1860 pink dress. Holds 1" boy and ¾" girl rag dolls looking at dog.

1969 *Hippy Man.* 2". (1)

Undressed Lady. 3". (1)
Lady Doll of 1830. 2½". (5) Shoulder head, old mache-type hairdo.
Easter Scene in Egg. 3¼" paper egg. (3) Wooded and rock landscape, six tiny animals peeking at 1" sleeping girl and boy rag dolls.
Doll Sal. 2". (20) A doll's doll.
Baby Topknot. 1¾". (35)
Baby Cry. 1-5/8". (60) Short dress. Two in 2½" straw clothes basket.
Madonna Carrying Baby. 1". Baby 5/16". (40)
Convention Visitor. 1". (89) *Dolly Bess* with pink straw hat, carrying doll and doll hat in tote basket.
Baby. 7/8". Wearing short dress. (17) In basket. (12) New features.
Baby. ¾". (24) Short dress.
Girl. ¼". (11)
Girl. 3/8". (16) Rags type heads.

1970 *Baby.* 1". (2) In rompers.
Rags Boy. 1". (3) Same as one carried by *Arms Full.*
Doll's Doll #3. ¾". (18)
Doll's Doll #4. ¾". Red yarn hair. (21) In locket. (8)
Doll's Doll #5. 11/16". Red yarn hair. (18) In locket. (5)
Sleepy Time. 1½". (14) Boy sleeping holds ½" teddy bear.
Teddy Bears. ¼". (4) Two white and two brown.
Teddy Bears. 1". (24) Brown felt.
Goldilocks and Three Bears. Girl 1¼". Bears 1¼-2¾". (3 sets)
Lady. 5½". (1) Mother Goose-type. Mobcap and dress.
Barefoot Fisher Boy. 1-7/8". (22) Whistling. Fish and pole.
Boy Lost. 1-7/8". (60) ca. 1908. Tears, ready to cry. Knap sack and 1" teddy bear.
Little Kate. 2". (38) Greenaway style with straw bonnet and 7/8" doll.
Betsy Two Face. 2". (72) ca. 1895. Change from laughing to crying by turning straw hat. Holds ¾" topsy-turvy doll with two heads, one good and one broken.
Me Doll. 2". (46) ca. 1912. From Irma Park photograph. Sitting on rug.

1971 *First Love.* 2". (20) Greenaway style. Boy and girl on bench, holding hands.
Cry Help. 1-5/8". (7) Holds 11/16" doll which a duck is trying to take.
Little Waif. 1-5/8". (12) Dress ca. 1860. Torn pinafore, one panty leg hanging down. Carries bedraggled 11/16" doll. Sad face.
Walking Dolly. 1-7/8". (26) *Little Mama* face and similar hairdo. White waist and green skirt. Holds 1-1/8" doll.
Queen Elizabeth. 1-7/8". (1) Elaborate costume.
Mr. and Mrs. Santa. 11". (3 pairs) In felt.
Mr. and Mrs. Santa. 1". (3 pairs)
Girl Rags. 1". (20) Ten in Easter egg scenes and ten in small boxes.

Angel. 1". (5)
1972 *Dolly Bess #2.* 1". (3) Red hair and green dress.
Doll Peg. 2". (3) A doll's doll.
Bunting. 1¾". (8) Same face as *Sleepy*; white suit and bunny ears.
Alice in Wonderland. 1-7/8". (1) With 1¼" rabbit.
Santa Mouse. 1¼". (4) In felt.
Puddle Duck. 1¾". (3) White felt, dress Beatrix Potter-style.
Cries of Paris Scene. 22 x 7 x 6". (1 scene) ca. 1600. Street with ten buildings 4-6" with merchandise in shops, 1" figures in period dress. Twenty-eight peddlers with wares and four upper class visitors.
Bear Scene. (1) Tree house with fourteen bears.
1973 *Mouse House.* (1) Six underground rooms all furnished, nine 1" dressed mice.
Bug Haven. 9½ x 12½ x 4". (1) Three underground levels with activity bugs.
Twins. 1½". (2 pairs) Boy and girl in Greenaway costume with ¾" doll and stick horse.
Baby Crying. 1-1/8". (2) Long dress.
Baby. 5/8". (2) Short dress.
Doll's Dolls. Boys 1½" and 1-9/16". Girls 1-1/8", 1-3/8", 1½", 1¾", 1-7/8", and 2". (2-5 each) All wax over porcelain heads, hands, and feet.

Catalog of B. Ravca Dolls

No catalog available.

Catalog of F. Ravca Dolls

Needle-sculptured fabric dolls with individually modeled head based on fabric. Woven label, "Made especially for you by Frances Diecks Ravca," sewn on skirt or pants.

1935-40 *Theatrical Characters.* From ballet, opera, operetta, and theatre.
1940 *Ballerinas and Premiers Danseurs.* 6-8". (over 100) Some representing actual dancers, most imaginative.
1944 *Springtime.* 12-14". (15) In St. George's OLD DOLLS.
1945 *Mary Margaret McBride.* 12". (1) 1940s radio personality. Presented to her.
1946 *Afghanistan Story Teller.* 23" when standing. (1 set) Group of three seated figures in St. George's DOLLS OF THREE CENTURIES.
1952 *Queens of England.* 36". (7 sets) Monarchs in their own right. Seven queens in each set. Widely shown and featured in the United States and Canada.
1968 *Primping.* 11". This is the "theme"–each doll is different.

Presidents' Wives. 20". (1 set) Strictly for display. Shown widely.

1973 *Easter Sunday.* 10". (many) Little black girl, dressed for Easter Parade with a Raggedy Ann doll. Each personality different.

Catalog of Thompson Dolls

Hand-carved wood figures with varying detail and different woods. Artist's signature (F.B. Thompson) and year carved on back of head or feet.

1968 *The Prophet.* 24". (1) Redwood. Carved beard and long hair.

Marianne Georgian. 22". (1) 24". (1) Redwood. Fully-jointed, glass eyes, carved hair and corset. Undressed.

Artist. 12". (1) Sugar pine. Sitting on a carved bench at easel. Ball-jointed, all wood. Carved dog watching.

Brother and Sister. 13". (1 set) Redwood. Ball-jointed, glass eyes, cloth bodies. Dressed 1850s.

Boy's Body like Shoenhuts. 15". (1) Sugar pine. Ball-jointed, tummy opens to show spring stringing system.

Victorian Man and Woman. 14". (1 pair) Wood. Carved and jointed.

1969 *Oriental Lady.* 22". (1) Redwood, hand-rubbed. White flowing robe.

Grandma Artist. 22". (1) Sitting on carved antique chair at easel. Carved hair with bandana, apron over shirt waist. Dog.

Nefertiti. 28". (1) All maple. Arms ball-jointed, sandals.

Grandma Perkins. 22". (1) 24". (1) Redwood head and hands. Beautiful head. 1915 costume. The twenty-two-inch doll carries a cane. The twenty-four-inch doll, a Bible.

Grandma Murphy. 22". (1) Redwood. Braids carved around ears.

Grandma Beulah. 22". (1) Redwood. Carved hair.

Minerva. 22". (1) Redwood. Carved handbag and boots, carries umbrella.

Samantha. 24". (1) Lovely carved hair and hat. Carved cane and Bible. Lavender blouse, dotted skirt.

Marianne Georgian. 22". (1) Light redwood. Carved coiled hair and corselet, turned waist. Undressed.

Cissy. 16". (1) Sugar pine. Carved head, hands, and feet; cloth body. Little girl in dotted Swiss.

Missy. 16". (1) Maple. Carved head, hair, hands, and feet; cloth body. Long-waisted lavender flowered dress and hair bow.

The Prophet. 24". (1) Redwood. Fully ball-jointed, carved beard and long hair. In Biblical clothes.

Li'l Nora. 18". White sugar pine. Fully ball-jointed, dainty carved hands, Mary Jane slippers, glass eyes, chubby legs.

Li'l Red. 8". (1) Redwood. Ball-jointed, large glass eyes, rotund tummy.

1970 *The Golfer.* 8". (1) Redwood. Ball-jointed. Little boy character. Tummy opens to show tiny carved heart on chain reading "To Sarah Barrett–with love."

Teddy Bears. 2-10". (70) Black walnut.

Rocking Horses. Scaled 1" to 1'. (45) Black walnut.

Man and Woman of 1840. 12". (1 pair) Sugar pine. Mortised joints.

Watchmaker. 24". (1) Redwood. Carved head, hands, and feet; cloth body. Table, tools of trade, and bench. Glasses. ca. 1900.

Woodcarver. 24". (1) Redwood. Carved head, hands, and feet. Handmade carving tools and tiny carvings on bench. Stool.

Artist. 24". (1) Redwood. Ball-jointed. Man with bald head, glasses, smock, tam, bench, easel, and paintbox.

Laughing Granny. 22". (1) Redwood. Carved head, hands, and feet; cloth body. Brown glass eyes, glasses. Dark brown dotted Swiss dress and white apron.

Roxanne. 24". (1) Redwood. Carved head, hands, and feet; cloth body. Blue glass eyes, Bible, purse. Very prissy in printed silk and hat.

Jillene. 14". (1) Basswood. Fashion figure. Carved high-heeled boots. Blue glass eyes, auburn wig, Gay Nineties dress, hat.

Jennifer. 14". (1) Basswood. Carved head, hands, and riding boots; cloth body. Brown glass eyes and red hair. 1905 bicycler in jodhpurs, white blouse with tiny tucks and teensy buttons, and white riding hat.

Ole Norwood. 20". (1) Redwood. Roguish old man. Carved hat, head, hands, and feet; cloth body. Pipe carved in left hand.

Lady of 1840. 12". (1) Redwood. Carved head, hands, and feet.

Li'l Irma. 15". (1) All wood. Carved head with gamin smile, poised hands, cute 1920 boots. Dressed in purple flowered long-waisted dress and cape.

Bonnet Doll, 1890 Style. 18". (1) Light redwood. Carved head, hands, and feet; cloth body. "Li'l Ole Lady." Braided hair. Quaint.

Peddler Doll. 24". (1) Redwood. Carved head, hair, and hands. Buttoned boots, basket of wares. Wrinkled clothes of 100-year old material.

Grandma Preston. 24". (1) Redwood. Carved hair, glasses, and veined hands. Glass eyes. In rocker.

1971 *Li'l Mabelle.* 16". (1) Basswood. Fully ball-jointed, glass eyes, wig, pink 1920 dress. Carved high-button shoes.

Li'l Meg. 16". (1) Sugar pine. Little girl. Ball-jointed, brown wig, tinted face, glass eyes. Middy blouse and skirt.

Teddy Bears. 10". (2) Maple. Ball-jointed. Masculine.

The Prophet. 24". (1) Cedar. Ball-jointed. Carved to look like Biblical prophet. Dressed in long robe.

Sunny. 8". (1) Redwood, ball-jointed. Gamin type, "googlie," high-buttoned shoes, pinafore.

Little Boy. 12". (1) Basswood. Carved head, hair, bare feet, and hands. Looking toward sky. Stained lightly.

Cigar Store Indian. 8". (4) Cedar, redwood, and pine. One piece.

Gaylon. 22". (1) Black walnut. One-piece carving of the First Pharmacist.

Captain Jinks of the Horse Marines. 18". (1) Cedar. One piece.

Li'l Nora. 16". Basswood head; composition body. Glass eyes, wig. Copy of body of original *Li'l Nora.*

1972 *Squattie Character Pigs.* 3". (1 set) Redwood burls, basswood, cedar, pine, and black walnut. Mama nursing 5 piglets. One-piece carvings. Many positions.

Li'l Nora. 16". (10) Dolly doll type. Carved head, each different, composition body copied from original in wood. Glass eyes.

Helene. 15". (1) Basswood. Ball-jointed, all carved. French type; French wig and dress.

Fred's Bru. 32". (1) Basswood. Ball-jointed, all wood. Glass eyes, auburn wig. French style velvet dress.

Penny Woodens. 6" and 8". (52) Sugar pine and willow. All carved, spoon hands, 1900-style boots, corset.

The Gossips. 18". (1 group) Redwood. Ball-jointed. All three "Li'l Ole Lady" characters. Varied positions on park bench: whispering, surprise, and giggling.

Lezah. 20". (1) Last redwood doll. Carved head, hands, and feet; cloth body. Flower peddler, smiling, sitting. 1900 print, apron, glasses.

1973 *Ole Fred the Wood Carver.* 24". (1) Poplar. Ball-jointed. The artist at perhaps age 70. Much character, lifelike, seated at carving bench. Dressed in plaid shirt, red vest, and beige pants.

Cigar Store Indians. 1". (3) Cherry. Miniatures.

The Prophet. 24". (1) Jellutong wood. Carved hair, beard, and moustache. Staff in hand, Biblical costume. Often called "Moses."

William DeLong. 24". (1) Jellutong wood. Portrait of last Civil War Veteran. Painted eyes, hair, brows. Miniature newspaper. Seated on bench.

Wood Carver–Sylvester Newton. 24". (1) Jellutong wood. Painted white hair, beard, moustache. Muscular arms and hands. Table with thirty carving tools.

Saddle Maker, "Shorty." 24". (1) Jellutong wood. Ball-jointed. Seated on cobbler-type three-legged bench with saddle.

The Winner's Circle. (1) Painted and stained one-piece carving of horse with ball-jointed jockey. Colors of jockey those of registered owner, Bernard Kaufmann of New York.

Li'l Lavina. *Li'l Sue.*
Li'l Ruth. *Li'l Jill.*
Evelena. *Francine.*

Each 16". Jellutong wood. Head carved different on *Li'l Nora.* Ball-jointed bodies. Dressed in long-waisted gathered or pleated dresses.

Googlie-Eyed Girl. 13". (1) Sugar pine. Ball-jointed body, wig, glass eyes. Undressed.

Googlie-Eyed Susie. 15". Cedar. Fully ball-jointed. Composition body, glass eyes, real hair wig. 1905 bathing suit.

Googlie-Eyed Erma. 16". (1) Basswood. Ball-jointed. Composition body, glass eyes, wig.

1974 *Little Ole Shoemaker.* 22". Jellutong. Fully ball-jointed. Shown working at cobbler's bench completely furnished in miniature tools, all hand-carved.

Roy August. 24". Jellutong. Ball-jointed. Quiet, refined gentleman, with pipe. Shown carving a carousel horse's head at fitted workbench.

Poverty Pearl. 16". (3) Jellutong. Carved head, hands, and feet. Raggedy patched dress, scraggly hair. Waif type.

Catalog of Elliott Dolls

No catalog available.

Catalog of Sweet Dolls

Bisque head, hands, and feet; muslin body stuffed with wool, later with sawdust. Exceptions as noted. Name and number incised in bisque.

1962 *Old Woman at Church.* 17". (2) Wax head, arms, and hands. Human hair wig. Holding rosary and carrying cane. Black lace shawl and apron.

Pedlar. 17". (1) Old woman adapted. Usual pedlar costume.

1963 *Milliner's Model Type.* 17". (1) Papier mache head; painted hair; kid body; wooden arms, hands, and legs. Three heads.

Old-Fashioned Girl. (1) Papier mache head for 28" doll.

1964 *Baby Albert.* 14". (5) Wax head, arms, and legs. Glass and painted eyes, pale silky curls of fur set in scalp for wig. Lace bonnet, white dress. Taken from primitive painting.

1965 *Sarah.* 19". (2) Wax head, arms, and legs. Glass eyes, muslin body stuffed with wool. Toddler in nineteenth century costume.

Boy. 18". (1) Wax head and arms. Mohair wig. From primitive painting.

1966 *Mercer Girl.* 16". (1) Bisque head, arms, and legs. Molded hair, sawdust-stuffed muslin body. Red challis dress, carrying carpetbag.

Girl. 9". (1) Bisque head, shoulder plate, arms, and legs.

Jennifer. 12". (10) Bisque head, arms, and legs. Blonde mohair wig.

1967 *Nora.* 23". (1) Bisque head, shoulder plate (swivel neck), arms, and hands. 1860 blue silk and embroidery dress.

Amy. 17". Bisque head, shoulder plate, and arms. Old mohair wig. Dressed late nineteenth century. Limit–10.

1968 *Julie.* 17". Bisque head, shoulder plate, and arms. Blonde mohair wig. Dressed late nineteenth century. Limit–10.

1969 *Beth Ann.* 18". Bisque head, shoulder plate, and arms. Dressed late nineteenth century.

1971 *Charles Edward.* Boy of seven. Unlimited.

1972 *Boy.* (1) Wax.

1973 *Laura.* Bisque head, shoulder plate, arms, and legs; cloth body. Child of four with distressed expression. After old photo.

Catalog of De Nunez Dolls

1940 *Woman.* 6". Carved wood, painted, articulated. Contemporary dress.

1947 *Woman.* 18". (2) Carved wood, painted. Calico dress, bonnet.

1949 *Woman.* 18". (1) Carved wood, painted. Bathing suit painted on.

Baby. 7½". (1) Carved wood, painted, articulated. White batiste and lace dress and bonnet.

1956 *Voodoo Dolls.* 18-21". (4 male, 2 female) Head and limbs of hard rock patching compound, enameled. Bodies of padded dowels. Males' hair molded; females', wigged.

1961 *Pedlar.* 21". Porcelain head and limbs, glass eyes, mohair wig. Dressed in dark green dress, white apron, mobcap, black hat, and red cape. #1 in artist's collection; limit–50.

1962 *Bergeret.* 24". Painted eyes, sculpted hair and shoes. Porcelain head and limbs; a few early dolls had cloth bodies, the rest kid. From portrait of Mme. Bergeret by Houdon. Dressed in Louis XVI style. Sold two dressed, the rest undressed. Limit–12.

1963 *Jasmine.* 14". Black child, glass eyes, mohair wig, cloth body. One pair dressed in 1890 style. Sold undressed. Limit–50.

Beau. Same as *Jasmine* with boy wig.

1964 *Pedlar.* 18". (41) A firedown of twenty-one-inch pedlar, same description.

1965 *Cyril.* 18". Man with skin wig, glass or painted eyes, kid body. In artist's collection: one Cyril unarticulated, painted eyes, dressed as a French Hussar; one dressed as gentleman of 1880. Doll sold undressed with pattern in style of 1880s available. Limit–50.

Catalog of Crosby Dolls

Porcelain head, hands, and feet on cloth body. China painted. Doll head signed "Diana Lence Crosby" and dated. Exceptions as noted.

1954-61 *Miss Unity Emblem.* 12". (250) Dressed in blue on black stand.

1959 *Abraham Lincoln.* 18". (12) On shoulder piece.

1960 *Clara Barton.* 18". (1) Portrait, brown glass eyes. Dress molded in shoulder.

1965-67 *Ye Boston Maid.* Special high-fire white glaze cap. Composite study of Pilgrim women. One thousand heads made for UFDC Boston Convention.

1967 *John Alden.* 20". (65) Molded Pilgrim hat, high-fire glaze.
Constance. 14". (35) Little Pilgrim girl with white glazed hat.
1968 *Edward.* 14". (35) Pilgrim boy with stocking cap.
1969-70 *Mlle. Detroit.* 18". Lady ca. 1835. Eight hundred heads for Detroit souvenir.
Country Boy. (1) Character.
City Boy. 12". (1) Character.
1971 *Deborah Crosby.* 12". (1) All bisque portrait at four. For grandmother.
1972 *Scarlett O'Hara.* 20". (6) Large molded hat.
1973 *The Belles of Fashion.* 12". (10) One-of-a-kind. Molded porcelain heads, applied or porcelain hats, bonnets with decorations.
1973-74 *Miss Teenager.* 12". "Helper" for Miami UFDC Convention, 1974.
Little Miss Sunshine. 12".

CATALOG OF HARRISON DOLLS

Porcelain head and arms; bodies cotton-stuffed muslin.

1949 *Ethel Shockley.* 18". (4) Portrait of her mother.
1958 *President and Mrs. Eisenhower.* 20" and 18". In inaugural dress.
1959 *Grace Kelly.* 20". In wedding dress.
Four Little Women. 18".
Elizabeth I. 16". (4)
Queen Victoria. 16". In later years.
Queen Elizabeth II and Philip. 18" and 20".
1960 *President Kennedy and Jacqueline.* 20" and 18".
President and Mrs. Lincoln. 20" and 16".
President and Mrs. Johnson. 20" and 18".
George and Martha Washington. 20" and 18".
Marian Harding. 8½". (250) Souvenir doll for Heart of Ohio Regional meeting. Mold broken.
1963 *Golden Years.* 19". Baby 4". Great-grandmother holding great-grandchild in long christening dress.
1964 *Godeyettes.* 18". Swivel heads with wigs. Different period dresses.
1967 *Nineteenth Century Dolls.* 13½". 1800 through 1900.
1970 *Felice.* 16". Little girl, blonde wig, dressed in white, 1900 period.

CATALOG OF HAINES DOLLS

No catalog available.

CATALOG OF ROMMEL DOLLS

No catalog available.

Catalog of Alleman Dolls

No catalog available.

Catalog of Nordell Dolls

No catalog available.

Bibliography

Bullard, Helen, THE TOY TRADER, Monographs

Roberta Bell, vol. 25, no. 3, April, 1972.
Frances Bringloe, vol. 25, no. 6, July, 1972.
Astry Campbell, vol. 22, no. 3, April, 1969.
Beverly Cerepak, vol. 24, no. 8, Jan., 1972.
Fern Deutsch, vol. 24, no. 2, March, 1971.
Herta Forster, vol. 25, no. 5, June, 1972.
Frank and Elizabeth Haines, vol. 25, no. 4, May, 1972.
Sharon Johnson, vol. 22, no. 5, June, 1969.
Wee Paulson, vol. 22, no. 4, May, 1969.
Madeline Saucier, vol. 25, no. 2, March, 1972.
Rose Sullo, vol. 25, no. 2, March, 1972.
Elizabeth Sweet, vol. 23, no. 3, April, 1970.

Sugg, Dr. Redding S. Jr., *Helen Bullard and the People Figures,* SOUTHERN VOICES, vol. 1, May-June, 1975.

Index

C

D

E

F

G

H

I

M

N

O

T